CHEWING GUM

CHEWING GUM

THE FORTUNES OF TASTE

Michael Redclift

ROUTLEDGE
NEW YORK AND LONDON

Published in 2004 by
Routledge
29 West 35th Street
New York, NY 10001
www.routledge-ny.com

Published in Great Britain by
Routledge
11 New Fetter Lane
London EC4P 4EE
www.routledge.co.uk

Routledge is an imprint of the Taylor and Francis Group.

Printed in the United States of America on acid-free paper.

10 9 8 7 6 5 4 3 2 1

Library of Congress Cataloging-in-Publication Data

Redclift, M. R.
Chewing gum : the fortunes of taste / Michael Redclift.
p. cm.
Includes bibliographical references and index.
ISBN 0-415-94418-X (HC : alk. paper)
1. Chewing gum—History. I. Title.
TX799.R35 2004
641.3'38—dc22
2003024771

CONTENTS

ACKNOWLEDGMENTS

Writing this book was made possible by a number of small grants, notably from the Central Research Fund of the University of London, and one large grant (grant RES_143_25_0007) from the Economic and Social Research Council (ESRC AHRB) of the United Kingdom, under the Cultures of Consumption research program directed by Dr. Frank Trentman. Dr. Oscar Forero, the researcher on the ESRC project and an invaluable colleague, took some of the best photographs. Oscar now knows much more about chicle than I do, and his book is on its way to being published! I owe a great deal to Dave McBride at Routledge, New York, for his painstaking work on the early drafts and his timely encouragement. Finally, my thanks go to my wife Nanneke for all her support, especially during our travels in Yucatán, and to all the people of the region, whose friendship and openness prompted me to write this book.

1

INTRODUCTION

"This gum," Mr Wonka went on, "is the latest, my greatest, my
most fascinating invention! It's a chewing gum meal! . . . Just a
strip of Wonka's magic chewing gum and that's all you'll ever need
at breakfast, lunch and supper! This piece of gum I've just made
happens to be tomato soup, roast beef and blueberry pie . . . !"

Willy Wonka in Roald Dahl's *Charlie and the Chocolate Factory*
(1964)

In true Manhattan fashion she's immaculately groomed. Then
she spits out her gum, and I remember where we are. Angelic as
she appears, Sarah Jessica Parker (of "Sex and the City" fame) is
a New Yorker. Here, even angels have attitude.

Eve MacSweeney, *Vogue* (February 2001)

She tells me about her husband, Harry Lewis. They were married for 57 years. "I lost him three years ago," she says, with the
air of someone who thinks she might find him again—down the
back of the sofa, or under the fridge. He played the saxophone.

"I don't think I thought much of him at first. He wooed me with chewing gum."

British wartime forces' "sweetheart" Vera Lynn, interviewed by Laura Barton for the *London Guardian* (October 11, 2001)

The British teenager who was found yesterday after going missing on a mountain in remote northern Queensland, Australia, last night spoke of the fear and hunger she endured during her three-day disappearance. . . . Equipped with a small bottle of water and a banana, which she ate on the first day, she survived on a packet of chewing gum for the rest of the time. "I'm always going to thank chewing gum for my survival," she said.

Report in *The Times* of London (November 30, 2002)

Is there any product with which you would *not* be associated?

News anchorman Jon Snow interviewing novelist Fay Weldon on the publication of her "sponsored" novel *The Bulgari Connection*, on British Channel Four News (September 4, 2001)

Wrigley's chewing gum might be a problem. . . .

Fay Weldon

Each of these quotations illustrates an important part of the story of chewing gum and the breadth of chewing gum's appeal and status as an icon of modern global society. Chewing gum is by turns habitual and regarded as a personal treat; it was, and is, a substitute for food, notably when food is unavailable. What began as a private, small indulgence developed into what is today sometimes labeled "medical confectionery." At the same time, chewing gum has conveyed desire in its associations with sex and the body. It has been used to express attitude, demonstrating coolness and sometimes even dissent to successive generations.[1]

What is perhaps most remarkable is that the appeal of chewing gum is in no way confined to the developed industrial world of North America, Europe, and Japan; it has penetrated developing markets with a ferocity and success equaled by very few products. Chewing gum long ago entered global culture, raising this most ordinary of products into an icon of modernity. (When the *Gemini V* astronauts went into space in 1965, each of their food packages contained two sticks of Trident sugarless gum, making chewing gum one of the few products that could lay claim to be galactic, rather than merely global.)[2] Today there are 550 companies making commercial gum in 93 countries throughout the world.

In Modernity's Shadow

Chewing gum is a recognizable emblem of mass consumer culture in the developed world. But the very modernity of gum—its ephemeral quality and its status as an easily replicable mass product—serves to obscure its origins and the primary economic relationship that underpins its market success. During most of the twentieth century, when chewing gum played an increasing part in so many peoples' lives, it was largely sourced from the southeastern region of Mexico, the Yucatán Peninsula in particular. Mexico's relations with the United States form the axis around which the chewing gum economy developed, and just as chewing gum represents modernity and consumer culture for the United States and most of the developed world, it came to represent premodernity and resource extraction for tens of thousands of families in the Yucatán.

This book tells the story of chewing gum, beginning with its invention and marketing in the late-nineteenth-century United States. But as we shall see, this narrative only makes sense against the backdrop of relations between the United States and Mexico at the time. The United States extended its territorial frontiers into what was Mexican soil after 1821, when Mexico gained independence from Spain. The growing confidence of the United States was matched south of the Rio Grande by turmoil, confusion, and increasing economic dependence on exports to the north. As the power of the United States increased, its anxiety about events in Mexico also increased, and it made efforts to ensure that European states recognized the Americas as a primary domain of influence for the United States. The geopolitics of hemispheric relations lies at the heart of the story of chewing gum.

At the same time, as I make clear in chapter 6, the business of chewing gum was founded on principles of mass consumption and popular taste that, although first developed in the United States, have come to characterize modernity at the beginning of the twenty-first century for the entire globe. Both its form and its cultural associations have mutated over time as well. Chewing gum gave birth to bubble gum (which was not sourced from Mexican resin) and bubble gum in turn served as a marker for other facets of consumer culture: bubblegum music, for example. Like chewing gum, it gave rise to merchandising strategies, such as baseball cards, that we recognize as the antecedents of product marketing today but that were in their infancy in the 1920s and 1930s. Today's celebrities routinely endorse products and, through their endorsement, lend their names to apparently unconnected items of consumption, like Pepsi-Cola and branded sportswear. Chewing gum's history helped lay the basis for this process. It was among the first of many products to link celebrities to a prosaic, everyday practice.

The final chapter investigates the latest stage in the career of gum. Chewing gum based on *chicle* is now treated as a sustainable forest product and hence is marketed to a new audience of consumers of natural organic products. While the production of chicle suffered a precipitous decline in the last half century, the production of gum from tropical forests is viewed today as an important potential constituent of sustainable forest ecology. Not only is the product natural, but also its production enables us to protect nature—no longer are such trees cut down for their timber. The growing importance of niche markets reflects new consumer preferences, which often are becoming increasingly progressive and green. Though impoverished forest workers in the Yucatán have harvested natural chewing gum for decades, its production has just now turned full circle. Chewing gum is likely to become a certificated product, and therefore comes with guarantees that it was traded fairly and has not degraded the environment. Finally, thousands of livelihoods are still made selling gum.

But before setting out on the story of chewing gum, let us consider one street salesman's experience, in the region from which gum was originally sourced, the Yucatán.

On the Street

I first met Pablo Ortega on the day that the president of Mexico visited Merida, the capital of Yucatán. It was early August and the police were cordoning off the main square, known popularly as the Plaza Grande. Hundreds of people were crowded into one corner of the huge plaza, some of them carrying banners and petitions for the restitution of some community privilege and others seeking to press crumpled pieces of paper into the president's hand, if they managed to get close enough to him. Many of those in the square that day merely turned up as dutiful supporters of the PAN, the pro-Catholic, right-of-center party that had controlled Yucatán since the early eighties and whose national president they were now receiving. Those who appeared either were dedicated *panistas* or were simply curious to see the president, but the latter group was clearly dominant.

Pablo Ortega worked on the streets as part of what development policy specialists call the "informal sector"; he is a street trader, a *changarrero,* selling sweets and chewing gum from a small tray that he carries.[3] He was selling sweets in little packets covered in gold paper and *topitos,* or corn chips. He also was selling chewing gum in several different varieties: gum that is good for the breath, sugar-free gum for the teeth, and just plain chewing gum to help wile away the time, doing nothing in particular. On this hot August day his tray was piled high with much more than he could reasonably hope to sell in a morning. He sold most gum, he told me, for between two and five pesos a stick, keeping between fifty centavos and a peso from each sale. It was, as they say, a tight margin.

He told me that business was very bad, that however much he sold was never enough, and that the price of everything but gum and sweets was going up. The arrival of the president was a small commercial opportunity, like many others, but only a small and temporary one. By the afternoon, the plaza would be packed with buses and cars again, the flags and banners would disappear,

Changarrero (street vendor) selling
chewing gum in Merida

Street vendor in Merida

and he would disappear just as surely into the throng of street vendors, beggars, touts, and workers returning home. The more established street vendors, the *changarreros* who sold from a stand (or *puesto*), had regular customers. The itinerant street salespeople, the *ambulantes* like him, went in search of customers, and found them, if necessary, at political demonstrations.

At one time, more than a century ago, the pavements of Merida had been lined with "gold" as well as street vendors. Most of the large, baroque, colonial-style buildings were built during the *henequen* boom, during the last decades of the nineteenth century. Henequen is a cactuslike plant that is a member of the *agave* family, which also produces tequila, Mexico's most famous drink and a recent beneficiary of global fashion in cocktails. (A cynic might reflect that, while removing government subsidies has served to undermine the income of much of Mexico's peasantry and to increase the numbers of itinerant street vendors, the process behind it, the liberalization of global markets, has also accelerated the demand for tequila, which celebrates market success.)

Henequen was referred to as "green gold" because, before the age of artificial fibers, it was used like sisal, for just about everything that needed a strong cord base, from rope to carpets and in boats and battle dress. It also was used for making hammocks, one of the great inventions of the Spanish Caribbean that have traveled the world. The word *hammock* was derived from Carib, the language of the people who lived there before Europeans arrived with their swords and diseases. When the Maya were being press-ganged into working on the henequen plantations and their white masters were building the stately mansions that line Merida's Paseo de Montejo, the Caribs were already an early casualty of history and empire. The hammock, unlike the Caribs, survived

Loading agave cactus used for making henequen

Merida today

A stately mansion that lines Merida's Paseo de Montejo

contact with the whites and eventually became part of their domestic kit, an essential accessory for life in the tropics.

Today people can dine well in the sepulchres of henequen: The
haciendas have mainly been turned into hotels and restaurants, visited by tourists, politicians, and visiting potentates when they come
to Yucatán. A century ago they were agro-industrial enclaves,
employing sweated labor, and were closer to Europe than to Mexico
City, economically if not geographically. The henequen hacienda
was a fiefdom ruled over by very powerful men whose names survived the Mexican Revolution of 1910 and still survive as street
names today. Henequen leaves its imprint in the curiously separate feeling that pervades the life and the culture of Yucatán:
detached from Mexico and much closer to the Caribbean, surviv-
ing and materializing in the jaded grandeur of a city with several
pasts. Each of these pasts was grafted onto the one before: The
Maya were admitted to the city from pueblos outside the city limits
and the *pueblos* became suburbs as the city expanded. The past is
also present in the material legacy of green gold (henequen): the
houses and squares that frame the wide streets where traders like
Pablo work today.

Near the center of the city is an old shop with a large sign outside, painted in bright colors. It reads "El Flaco y El Gordo" ("the
skinny one and the fat one," both terms of affection). The manager
is Jaime Soler, who talks with enthusiasm about his business. He
sells chewing gum wholesale to the *changarreros* of all types, and
mainly he sells the popular cheaper varieties of branded, packaged gum, like the original Chiclets, and the more upmarket
Adams's brands, such as Clorets. This represents an important
part of his regular business. He collects new stock at intervals
from the manufacturers in Mexico City and elsewhere in Mexico.

Interior of chewing gum shop in Merida

Exterior of shop

In his shop the best-selling brands are presented at eye level, on shelves about four feet six inches from the floor, for the Mayan people are usually very short, even by Mexican standards. The height of the shelves, he points out, is quite deliberate. The brands with more popular or common appeal, especially to children, are located on even lower shelves. But much of his business goes to customers who buy chewing gum in novelty form for distributing at children's parties or for stuffing into piñatas, the papier-mâché figures that Mexicans fill with small presents and sweets and ritually smash at children's parties and on special occasions, such as Christmas. The continuing importance of piñatas ensures that there is still a steady sale for gum in this form.

In Mexico novelty toys with chewing gum ingredients are so rich and varied they almost defy description. There are model planes and cars as well as houses and animals that are made of plastic but contain the estimable gum. If a consumer's taste runs to more exotic images, he or she will not be disappointed. Consumers can buy fierce animals, mythical beasts, and plastic scorpions with gum in them. Also available are baby's bottles with small balls of gum inside, surgeon's implements, filled with gum, and long sticks of tutti-frutti gum. (The expression *long sticks*, by the way, refers to sticks up to a meter in length.)

In Mexico today, there is almost nothing that one learns as a small child about play and the outside world, about celebrities, about sports and celebrations, and about the family that does not find its apotheosis in chewing gum. Chewing gum, oddly enough, functions as a material celebration of life itself. Indeed, there are few celebrations, fiestas, or saints' days that do not call for, and get, a commemoration in chewing gum.

Interior of chicle cooperative store today

Points of Departure

The story of chewing gum may start in a square in tropical Mexico, but it does not end there, as I make clear in this book. Indeed, there could be other starting points to this story. It might begin with the self-made entrepreneurs who developed commercial chicle-based gum in the United States, or the Maya who fought to control the forests in which the chicle was harvested. For many the story begins with the American GIs who chewed gum as part of their daily ration during the Pacific campaign of World War II, having already introduced it to England. After the war chewing gum entered much of what had been the European Theater.

There are many separate ingredients in the story of chewing gum, but three stand out as essential, having come to represent almost timeless elements in the bigger picture. The first ingredient is the importance of chewing gum to taste and popular culture, including the mass marketing of brands and customized images of consumption in the United States. Chewing gum was among the first mass-produced products of the twentieth century. Such items typically associated everyday life with either the exotic or the icons of national esteem—sports stars, movies, and public monuments. I tell this part of the story in chapters 2, 5, and 6. The second ingredient is the way in which chewing gum came to represent, and to characterize, the relations between Mexico and the United States for more than a century. This relationship lies at the heart of this book, and I discuss it in chapter 3. The third part of the story is bound up with the tropical forest frontier and the role of extractive industries in its maintenance and depletion. This was the case in the past, but it is equally true today, as these forests disappear under the chain saw and the bulldozer. I examine this part of the history in chapter 7.

Chewing gum thus speaks to us today in the different vocabularies of both custom and novelty. With regard to the former, it is iconic of all things American in the United States and much of the rest of the world. South of the border, though, there is another narrative: as the dark side of a long history of ecological and social exploitation, a native product that is now being increasingly relegated to peoples' memories.

Chewing gum left behind a rich history that remains largely unexplored, one that cannot be pigeonholed. Its rise was associated with growing preeminence of the United States. The early chewing gum entrepreneurs made innovations in marketing and public relations. A product that was virtually without value became a valued totem of the American way of life. The story is also about material transformations. To meet the needs of the new market in the United States, people transformed the forests and livelihoods of southeast Mexico, bringing in new forms of political organization and providing the funds for Mayan cultural resistance. Chewing gum had been used by the ancient Maya and subsequently by the armies of the Mexican Republic in the nineteenth century. Later it was to fuel the servicemen and servicewomen from the United States in wider battle arenas, during and after World War II.

But the story does not end there. Today a new vocabulary has emerged that places "natural" chewing gum on a cultural pedestal as a sustainable forest product and even, remarkably, as a symbol of hope for a more sustainable future.

THE "AMERICAN INVENTION"

The American love affair with chewing gum has a narrative sweep like that of other better-known products, such as gasoline, spices, and coffee, although its use was not so immediately obvious. Indeed, chewing is an often overlooked aspect of everyday life, despite its ubiquity. But the development of the product that made chewing easy—and enjoyable—opened up an extraordinary series of events. The history of chewing gum is bound up with some of the most important facets of American society in the late nineteenth century, and it played at least a small part in the cultural globalization of the twentieth century.

The story of chewing gum is linked to several processes that came to characterize the early twentieth century in the United States: the rise of family entrepreneurs on the East Coast, the widening of the market for everyday items of consumption in the migrant cities and rural hinterland, and the development of popular taste and, with it, cultural icons. The mythology of gum, which is part and parcel of this history, reflects a series of socio-economic trends that pushed the United States to the forefront of the world stage in the 1920s.

But it all began under very peculiar circumstances. Following an improbable meeting in 1869, two people from very different worlds introduced chewing gum to the United States. The first person was General Santa Anna, the former president of Mexico, who was famous in the United States as the victorious general at the battle of the Alamo in 1836. Although no Americans escaped with their lives (including Davy Crockett), it was a Pyrrhic victory for the Mexican army. Shortly afterward, Texas gained its independence from Mexico.

The second man was Thomas Adams, a former military photographer and inventor who, in 1869, was living with his wife and seven children in New York City. The circumstances of the meeting of Santa Anna and Adams in New York—the primal event in the history of chewing gum—requires some background explanation. It also requires a historical detour via the battles of the Alamo and San Jacinto, which turned the tide against Mexico and served to define its territorial integrity for posterity. For the story of chewing gum is very much a Mexican–American affair.

"The Napoleon of the West"

Santa Anna's periods as leader of an independent Mexico were among the most disastrous in the country's recorded history. Born on February 21, 1794, he began his career as an officer in the Spanish army, but at the time of Mexican independence in 1821,

Continental

Territory of Alta California

Treaty

Territory of Nuevo Mexico

N

Sonora y
Sinaloa

Line

Sabine River

(Louisiana)

Pacific

Coahuila y Texas

Chihuahua

Gulf of California

Gulf
of
Mexico

Territory of
Baja California

Durango

Nuevo
Leon

Zacatecas

Tamaulipas

Ocean

San
Luis
Potosi

Guanajuato

Mexico City

Jalisco

Michoacan

Yucatan

The United States
of Mexico,
1824

Mexico

Puebla

Veracruz

Tabasco

Oaxaca

Chiapas

Soconusco

Mexico's borders in 1824

he joined the revolution under Iturbide, its leader. He gradually emerged as a leading political figure, after turning against and helping to overthrow Iturbide. In 1829 he was hailed as the "Hero of Tampico" after helping to defeat an invading army that landed in the Gulf of Mexico, and he officially became president of the new republic in 1833, at the age of thirty-nine. Santa Anna tried to enforce centralized control over the various regions of Mexico, but they recoiled at his suppression of all dissent. In 1836 he moved against the rebellion in Texas in an attempt to quell the "Texians," a motley population that recently had been augmented by immigration from the United States to the north.

The Mexican army was relatively well trained, but communications were poor, and Mexican victory at the fort known as the Alamo against a poorly equipped army of 183 defenders proved to be temporary. However, the effect of the defeat sent a shock wave across Texas and the United States to the north. Sam Houston, commander in chief of the Texas army, left Washington for the scenes of the various skirmishes between Santa Anna's forces and the Texan defenders. News of the Alamo slaughter terrified the population of the newly settled province, and many people packed their belongings into wagons and carts and fled their homes for the Louisiana border in fear that Santa Anna's forces would occupy their homesteads and exterminate them. Known in Texan history as the "Runaway Scrape," the drama of their plight immediately stiffened the resolve of the Texan army—and its supporters to the north.

Houston, realizing that his few hundred troops were no match for the Mexican army, marched down the east bank of the Colorado River, near the present-day town of Columbus. But fifty miles to the south of them, a volunteer army had paid a heavy price for defeat at the hands of General Jose Urrea's Mexican forces who, on Palm Sunday 1836, marched the Texan volunteers onto the road and brutally dispatched them on the express orders of Santa Anna. The Texan army was still in retreat and was suffering from desertion, but Houston rallied the troops who remained and, spurred on by a caustic note from provisional Texas president David G. Burnett urging a more aggressive stance, eventually returned to the fray. In the meantime, while the retreat proceeded, the interim Texan government fled, eventually to Galveston on the Gulf coast, with Santa Anna in pursuit.

Many of Houston's officers and men, as well as government officials, believed that his strategy was to lead the pursuing Mexicans to the Sabine River, the eastern border of Texas, where U.S. troops, under General Pendelton Gaines, were camped. From a captured Mexican prisoner it was learned that the Mexican forces had burned Harrisburg and had gone down the west side of the bayou, with Santa Anna in overall command. The blue-uniformed Mexican army had, in fact, made camp under high ground overlooking a marsh, about three-fourths of a mile from the Texan camp. At 3:30 in the afternoon on April 21, 1836, Houston readied his men for battle. They could hear little from the Mexican army, and it was assumed most of the men were enjoying their customary siesta. In fact, at the start of the campaign, Santa Anna amazed his subordinates with his attention to detail. On April 21, however, like Napoleon at Waterloo only a couple of decades earlier, he had apparently lost his focus completely. Legend has it that he retired to his tent with the voluptuous mulatto slave Emily Morgan (the famed "Yellow Rose of Texas") and his personal opium chest. Santa Anna was otherwise engaged when the enemy struck.

The movements of the Texan army were screened from the Mexican troops by trees and the high ground, and it was soon clear that Santa Anna had neglected to post lookouts. Once they were given the command to advance, the Texan patriots moved quickly out of the woods and over the rise. After forty days of guarded retreat in the field, they were prepared for action and went forward to meet the Mexican army in what must have looked like a bizarre military movement. Only one company of the nine hundred men who fought for the Texan army, the Kentucky Rifles, wore uniforms. The majority of the troops were a rough assembly of homesteaders and hardened frontiersmen. Legend has it that they went into action with the cry of "Remember the Alamo!" ringing out as they opened fire. Much of the fighting that ensued was hand-to-hand combat, and it resulted in the total destruction of the Mexican forces, as the Texans pursued them relentlessly. The battle itself lasted only eighteen minutes. Eventually, the fugitive Mexican army fled into the marshes, where many drowned, and the river is said to have run red with blood. The Mexican troops were slaughtered unmercifully, despite Houston's intervention, in retaliation for the massacres suffered by the Texans at the Alamo and other skirmishes.

Santa Anna had, in his inimitable way, managed to escape from the scene of the battle. The following day Houston ordered a thorough search for him, and eventually he was found hiding in the long grass. He wore a common soldier's apparel—round jacket, blue cotton pantaloons, skin cap, and soldier's shoes. However, on his way back to the Texan camp, various Mexican prisoners recognized their former leader and cried, "El presidente!", immediately betraying his identity. Santa Anna was brought before General Houston, who was sitting under the headquarters' oak tree and nursing a foot injured by a rifle ball earlier in the battle. The Mexican president was as imperious as ever and declared that he was "none other than General Antonio Lopez de Santa Anna, and a prisoner of war currently at your disposition." Frightened that the Texan troops might lynch him, he pleaded for treatment appropriate to that of a prisoner of war: "You can afford to be generous," he is reported to have said, "You have captured the Napoleon of the West!"

Through interpreters the Texan and Mexican leaders talked for nearly two hours, during which time Santa Anna availed himself of the familiar painkiller being administered to the wounded Houston. A mellow conversation ensued for the rest of the afternoon, with the two men basically dividing up North America while stoned on opium. Santa Anna agreed to the complete Mexican evacuation of Texas and eventually to Texan independence.

But Santa Anna, far from leaving history at this point, proved to be a serial adversary of the United States as well as a flawed hero to his fellow countrymen. Indeed, there are few leaders in history who experienced as many ups and downs as Santa Anna. By 1838 he was back in the Mexican army again, and lost a leg defending Veracruz from French attack. He became president again until 1845, when he was exiled to Cuba for incompetence. During the Mexican–American War in 1846 and 1847, and after several lucky escapes, he was eventually restored to power in Mexico City, with U.S. support. (The title 'Napoleon of the West' seemed appropriate.) He then turned against the United States and returned to exile when the Americans took Mexico City in 1848. Santa Anna still was not finished, however. In 1853 he was recalled to the presidency and was exiled again in 1855. A few years later, in 1864, he tried to persuade the United States to support him against the Emperor Maximilian, who had become the French puppet ruler of Mexico. Yet, at the same time, he offered his services to Maximilian himself. Not without reason, both sides turned him down.

Despite the twists and turns of diplomacy and his Machiavellian maneuvers to retain power in Mexico, with or without U.S. support, Santa Anna found asylum in the Big Apple. Five years later, in 1869, at age seventy-five, he was living temporarily in Staten Island, New York. Santa Anna was still a man with grand ambitions, but his credibility and morale were low. This is where Thomas Adams and his eldest son met him, and it marks a watershed in the history of chewing gum.

The Staten Island Agreement

This improbable turn of events, which brought together a leading Mexican general and an obsessive Yankee inventor, provided both parties with an opportunity to demonstrate their capacity for entrepreneurship. The other man at the meeting on Staten Island could hardly have been more different from Santa Anna. Thomas Adams was a man for whom inventing things was almost second nature. He had been orphaned at the age of nine, and this experience had taught him to be self-sufficient. During the American Civil War he had served as a military photographer, taking formal photographs of ordinary soldiers, who sent them home to their families. Even the challenges of the new art of photography could not contain his ardor for the new and the inventive. He proceeded to make a variety of gadgets and devices, such as a novel feed bag for horses and a special burner for kerosene lamps, but only a few had any commercial success. Somewhat discouraged, in 1869 Adams bought a glass shop one block from the Staten Island ferry dock. One day Adams was visited by a man named Rudolph Napegy, with whom he formed a friendship. Napegy offered to introduce Adams to somebody he described as his boss, a Mexican general who held the key to a potentially important invention. The man was Antonio Lopez de Santa Anna.

By this time Santa Anna was in ailing health, white haired, and partially deaf. In keeping with his long-standing ambitions, he told Adams that he needed enough money to finance a Mexican army of liberation to overthrow the existing government. Given the circumstances in Mexico at the time, this plan was more than faintly ludicrous. Santa Anna hoped to raise the money by selling quantities of latex, called *chicle* in Spanish, derived from the *chicozapote* tree, which was native to the Yucatán Peninsula, a part of Mexico that he had visited in 1867.[1] The Mexican forces he led at San Jacinto had chewed chicle, and it was highly valued by the troops. The Maya of the region also chewed it and used it for ceremonial purposes since time immemorial. However, while chicle sold for only five cents a pound, crude rubber, which was increasingly used for the tires of carriages, sold for about $1 a pound. Santa Anna presented Adams with a large lump of gray dirt, covered in bark and stones. This dirt was chicle, and he was confident that its rubberlike qualities could earn them both a fortune in the form of rubber tires.

Adams immediately rose to the challenge and arranged to import a ton of the substance from Mexico. For several months he employed his family in trying to convert this springy sap into something resembling vulcanized rubber, but to no avail. Furious that he was being kept waiting, Santa Anna lost patience with Adams's experiments and disappeared from his life. He could hardly have suspected that the unusual substance with which Adams was experimenting would ultimately make many Americans vast personal fortunes and, even more surprisingly perhaps, play an important role in the history of warfare throughout the following century.

It was not long before another event occurred that was to affect the grand designs of both the military man and, the aspiring inventor. After almost a year spent trying to transform the chicle into something useful, Adams went into a drugstore in New York and overheard the shopkeeper selling a young girl a penny's worth of chewing gum. According to one of Adams's sons, Horatio, his father then asked the storekeeper what kind of chewing gum the child had bought. The man replied that it was "pretty poor gum," called Curtis White Mountain, and was derived from paraffin wax. Adams, realizing that his gum had an unexpected use, persuaded the storekeeper to try an alternative chewing gum and, on returning home, he immediately went into production.

The gum that the little girl bought was the immediate antecedent of chicle-based gum, and it had been developed in response to public demand for gum derived from spruce resin. Curtis White Mountain was named after John Baker Curtis. By the time he had entered the chewing gum story, spruce gum was already a well-established favorite in the United States. The American Indians, and the European settlers who imitated them, had long been in the habit of chewing on the resin from spruce trees. As the timber industry in the United States made deeper inroads in the native forests, lumbermen began to collect and sell the spruce resin for extra income. Curtis's invention brought entrepreneurial flair to what was already a common practice: By packaging spruce resin and retailing it under his name, he made a natural product into a commercial one. Using his own family's labor, Curtis boiled up batches of resin, skimmed off the bark and twigs, rolled it into a slab, and then cut it into strips that were covered in cornstarch to stop them from sticking together.

These strips of gum were the first to prove a real commercial success. He priced them at two for a penny, and the young Curtis set out to sell them to storekeepers from his home in Bangor, Maine. The first stores to stock Curtis's gum immediately sold out, and Curtis's State of Maine Pure Spruce Gum was soon an enormous success. In the first year of production he made $5,000, and by 1852 he had built the world's first chewing gum factory in Portland. Spruce resin did not prove to be the best ingredient for making gum, however. Its natural taste was not particularly pleasant, and the trees from which it was derived were already dwindling in supply. Consequently Curtis moved onto gums derived from paraffin wax, which were sweetened with flavors such as vanilla and licorice.

Adams's gum had chewing qualities that were clearly superior to Curtis's gum. Chicle could be turned into the consistency of putty and rolled into balls. In February 1871 the shop in New Jersey sold out of the tasteless chicle, and it placed orders for more. Adams formed the second batch into strips, as Curtis had done, and wrapped the sticks in brightly colored tissue paper. Two hundred of these sticks were packaged in a box featuring a color picture of New York's City Hall and were called "Adams New York No. 1—Snapping and Stretching." Unknowingly several of the conventions of gum merchandising were already being laid down in popular culture: ease and novelty in its use, associations with wider cultural and historical landmarks, and attractive gimmicky packaging.

Another element of the story, which Adams exploited like Curtis before him, was to take the product on the road. Chewing gum was sold to the public wherever the public could be found, and in this it resembled the products sold by other itinerant sales-people in this period.[2] Initially shopkeepers were not enthusiastic about stocking the gum, but Adams managed to leave it with them on consignment, for sale or return. So successful was this marketing that a company was formed, Adams and Sons, in 1871, and they set up a small factory employing young women as packers. In the same year Adams invented a gum making machine that kneaded the chicle like dough and then flattened it into thin strips. He experimented next with flavored gum and, as chicle does not easily absorb flavors, Adams added dried root bark from the sassafras tree. He also shredded licorice into the chicle, turning it black, and made the celebrated Black Jack gum (a version of which can still be bought today).

Other entrepreneurs soon arrived on the scene, inspired by Adams's evident success. One of these entrepreneurs was John Colgan, a pharmacist from Kentucky, who added powdered sugar and a spicy sap, tolu, which was used at the time in cough medicines. Colgan's Taffy-Tolu Chewing Gum was an overnight sensation when it was introduced in 1880. Colgan sold his drug-store and built another gum manufacturing plant. Again, he took his product to the streets, where boys sold it from bicycles and horse trolleys. Within a year his example was followed by ten other companies, selling similar products to a public whose imagination and interest had risen to a feverish pitch. Meanwhile, Adams had invented a gum vending machine, which he installed on the elevated train platforms of a New York City station, and which was filled with tutti-frutti gumballs. Adams advertised this product along Broadway through strategically placed billboards. Previously the reputation of chewing gum had been communicated by word of mouth alone; now it entered the domain of mass advertising in public spaces. And this was how chewing gum became emblematic of style and popular taste in the twentieth century.

Selling the Commonplace and the Habitual

By the late nineteenth century, the United States was home to a burgeoning collection of small-scale entrepreneurs, all hoping to make a good living from their own brands of chewing gum. A native of Indiana named Jonathan P. Primley exploited the potential sex appeal of something you put in your mouth with a gum called Kis-Me, while a Cleveland druggist, Edward E. Beeman, invented a gum that incorporated a pepsin compound. Claiming that it was a cure for heartburn, Beeman's unfortunate choice of a pig for his wrapper design did little for his sales. It was soon evident that the way in which gum was wrapped was almost as important as the gum itself.

By 1900, chewing gum was already using what have become the commonplace elements in mass advertising and communication: billboards in public spaces, innovative packaging, and strong cultural associations with places. William White added another element in 1898 in the form of the celebrity: linking the identities of famous people with the gum the customer chewed. White hit on the idea of adding mint flavors to corn syrup, making his gum an immediate success. However, the most remarkable thing about White's career was the way he combined public celebrity with new technologies to market his product. Visiting England, he managed to press a stick of his Yucatán gum into the hands of a bewildered Prince of Wales (later Edward VII). We can only imagine what Edward thought of this gesture at the time, but we know with certainty that White exploited this sales pitch immediately. He cabled the United States from London to say that he had introduced the future British sovereign to his gum and that it had been an instant success. This kind of audacious publicity was to mark chewing gum from the turn of the twentieth century onward.

When Thomas Adams finally retired as president of Adams and Sons in 1899, at the age of eighty-one, he left his family a fortune. By the time of his son's death in 1926, this amounted to more than $2 million, equivalent to about $30 million today. Adams senior had taken a lump of chicle and invested $35 of his own savings in its commercial transformation into edible gum. This would become the basis for most chewing gum in the first half of the twentieth century, and it lasted until synthetics were introduced at the time of the Korean War. But the contribution of people like Adams and Curtis also affected more broad economic and political relations, of which they could only be dimly conscious. Dramatic changes were taking place in American society in this period, which facilitated and enabled mass advertising and popular taste to play a leading role. At the same time in neighboring Mexico, the country of Santa Anna, the American taste for chewing gum derived from chicle was a potent factor in the transformation of the Mexican forest frontier.

Despite the skepticism and disapproval of powerful social classes, popular taste has set the cultural tone more often than not in the modern era. As Sidney Mintz observed, new ingredients in the diet, like sugar and sugar products, provided opportunities for the creation of new everyday rituals, whose regularity comported with new notions "of fitness, rightness, and validation."[3] They sometimes mark breaks in the world of work, opportunities to lay down tools and create new rituals around leisure. They also mark opportunities to share recreational time with others. Societies create such rituals using the ingredients at hand. Take the literary example of Mark Twain's Tom Sawyer sharing his (spruce) gum "turn about" with Becky Thatcher in the Missouri of the late 1840s. The sharing of a piece of gum—passing it from one to another—became part of kids' ritual in mid-nineteenth-century America.[4]

At the same time, the advent of commercially produced gum raised other questions that lay at the heart of contemporary discussions of personal consumption. The consumption of gum, like other food choices, was linked not merely to outlay and to monetary cost but to the displacement of other activities—to the idea of free time during the working day. Chewing gum could be undertaken at virtually *any time* and in *any place,* which held an obvious appeal to an increasingly busy society. It was an activity with obvious appeal for the itinerant and opportunistic. This very "everydayness" enables gum to be integrated into the sinews of daily life. Chewing gum was thoroughly mundane, yet enjoyable. And because of its convenience, it also was potentially *habitual.*[5]

If ritual and habit were important elements in the growing appeal of commercial chewing gum, then in what sense can we describe its consumption as unnecessary or unfunctional, for either the economy or the society of the nineteenth-century United States? The point about American life in this period is that the rules were, to some extent, new ones. This was well understood by foreign observers. The shrewd French critic Alexis de Tocqueville had observed that American society in the 1830s was markedly different from that of Europe. He noted that, unlike in most European countries, the imagination of America's poor was "haunted . . . by the desire of acquiring the comforts of the world. . . . They are therefore always straining to pursue or to retain gratifications so delightful, so imperfect, so fugitive."[6] Chewing gum, an American invention, was a perfect exemplar: It incorporated instant gratification into everyday life.

The Vernacular Culture of Late-Nineteenth-Century America

This search for gratification was not confined to America, of course, nor was its fulfillment. But in other respects, chewing gum illustrated a quality in American life, which Tocqueville was quick to see. He observed that Americans were more "conversant with the principles of true freedom than most of their European contemporaries." These libertarian—if not quite democratic—impulses were celebrated through an enjoyment in what we have come to call vernacular culture, things that are endemic to a place, local, native. Chewing gum had been part of Native American life and, as we have seen, that of the ancient Maya. In America chewing gum was tolerated in a way that it was not in Europe, even after World War II. It provided cheap, unalloyed pleasure, and it could be shared. Gum chewing added a dimension to sociability and did not require approval. The notion that it was somehow disrespectful to chew gum, although not unknown in the United States, was much more common in Britain and Europe.

The usefulness—or otherwise—of some aspects of personal consumption is also a heavily contested idea. The debate is indicative of the need to provide moral justifications for human action that is not evidently altruistic or productive. A number of obvious points need to be made at the outset. First, it is clear that what is considered normal consumption behavior changes radically over time: in the mid-eighteenth century it was abnormal to be served more than two meals a day in England, or three in France. Normality in daily habits varies widely between societies and over time.

If normality in consumption is not fixed, then neither is the idea of extravagance. Consumption that is looked upon as extravagant—and the boundaries of extravagance—can shift very abruptly with changes in taste and consumer power. Commentators on fashion have suggested that the "new look" after World War II, which swept women's fashions, with its apparently extravagant use of material and longer hemlines, came about as a reaction to the privations of wartime and the availability of cloth. Under such circumstance extravagance was seen as a virtue, not a vice. Other social critics have inveigled against specific areas or items of personal consumption demonstrating extravagance, as Thorstein Veblen did in the case of people who employed domestic servants. More recently, some writers have brought passion to bear on the evident lack of modesty and thrift exhibited by modern consumer society. J. K. Galbraith, for example, in *The Affluent Society* famously criticized the "big, ungainly, unfunctional" automobiles and pointed up the contrast between private extravagance and public squalor.[7]

Stanley Lebergott, in his work on American patterns of consumption, commented that consumption has always reflected the sum of things hoped for, rather than "the evidence of things seen." In his view, our consumption says as much about aspiration as about material possession. Many of the things that people enjoy doing most have little to do with their physical survival, although they contribute to their overall sense of well-being. They are not functional in a literal sense but may celebrate living, or life itself.[8] On the other hand, unlike many of the items discussed by Stanley Lebergott, chewing gum clearly does provide a measure of direct satisfaction, rather than indirect, anticipatory pleasure. Chewing gum celebrates a bodily function in an immediately pleasing way, unlike many other forms of consumption that are more indirect but are no less necessary. The interesting thing about chewing gum is that, though its pleasure content is so immediate and so material, it has also become invested with the stuff of dreams. As we shall see, chewing gum makers and consumers have all lived out a fantasy rooted in a bodily function that is universal but that passed from the United States to the world through the medium of the market. There are many forces shaping human happiness, and economic welfare is just one of them. It is tempting, then, to see chewing gum as a way of celebrating contentment, if not actually a way of achieving it. While it is an item of everyday consumption, our genes do not demand it nor does it work in our financial interest. But does this make it any less socially necessary? Whether or not it is "socially necessary," chewing gum, for those who enjoy it, satisfies a human need every bit as important to the economist's "utility function."[9]

Chewing and Social Change

The society in which commercial chewing gum made an appearance—in late-nineteenth-century America—was one undergoing a massive social transformation. Between 1830 and the outbreak of World War I in 1914, the United States changed from a largely agrarian country, with apparently limitless farmland, to the leading industrial power of the twentieth century. The urban population grew remorselessly during this period until, by 1920, more people lived in towns than in the country. These cities became the proverbial melting pots, where immigrants from a host of cultures as well as their children produced a new, polyglot culture. On top of this, between 1870 and 1910 the workforce had almost doubled to about 33 million working men and women.

During the peak years of migration to the United States, the combined population of foreign-born workers and their children made up 45 percent of the population. It was immigrant families who provided the service workers for the growing American middle class: the laundresses, scrub women, and maids. The men found work in the expanding iron and steel industries, in automobile manufacturing, and in the clothing industry.[10] Small-scale entrepreneurialism, which had dominated the U.S. economy up to the mid-nineteenth century, was fading in the face of corporate capitalism. But in immigrant ghettoes such entrepreneurialism was still vital, evidenced by greengrocers, fishmongers, and ethnic-goods manufacturers. Within these neighborhoods everyday life reflected traditional values: food, clothes, and religious observation and ritual. Immigrants lived around a familiar world of the local store, meeting room, church, and market. But increasingly American society hybridized, and immigrants assimilated fairly rapidly, usually within two generations of arrival.[11]

There were sweeping cultural changes afoot as well. Chewing gum made its appearance at a time when the United States was opening up, in an unprecedented way, to a variety of new fads and popular remedies. The list is like a roll call of twentieth-century addictions and popular belief in medical cures: Herbalism, homeopathy, hydropathy, osteopathy, chiropractic, and electric shock treatment all had numerous enthusiasts at this time. In addition, many of the new cures and popular practices involved imbibing (or refraining from) food or liquids. Temperance, vegetarianism, mineral water cures, cereal consumption, organic foods, vitamins, and dieting all made their appearance on a popular scale, in the late nineteenth and early twentieth centuries.[12] What people put in their mouths and stomachs was not merely an act of passive consumption but a statement about what we would today call "lifestyle."

One of the most bizarre and interesting examples of popular habits in this period was the movement instigated by Horace Fletcher to encourage people to chew their food more assiduously. Fletcher was born in Massachusetts in 1849, but he made his fortune importing Japanese art, toys, and novelties, as well as by selling printer's ink. At the age of forty he was already a rich man and possessed almost limitless energy and boundless personal curiosity. In addition to being rich, he was an epicure and a charmer, according to contemporary accounts. Despite an athletic past, his love of good food and wine and the ability to indulge his taste, led Fletcher to put on weight. At the age of forty-four his obesity meant that he was denied life insurance, and this experience effectively changed his life. Searching the ideas of the day for the key to contentment and a healthy life, Fletcher hit on the act of chewing.

In *The A, B to Z of Our Own Nutrition* (1903), he argued that most diseases, pain, and worry were caused by indigestion or the "mal-assimilation" of food. Digestion, he argued, began in the mouth; if people did not chew their food properly, they did not produce saliva, and this watering of the mouth produced the true

or earned appetite that helped to keep people healthy. Fletcher
thus brought together two vital ingredients of American popular
culture: an optimistic, individualistic outlook of positive thinking
and a clear, even obsessive, concern with the body. Fletcher
invented, in effect, a theory of mastication.[13]

The followers of Fletcher believed passionately that food
should be chewed until its taste had been completely exhausted, a
process that could be very time-consuming. Correct chewing, a
process that came to be known as Fletcherizing, involved keeping
the food in the mouth for at least thirty seconds after it had been
liquefied. This required a lot of concentration on the part of the
chewer and could lead to protracted periods of silence. (It was
also something of a social embarrassment, especially at dinner
parties where the company was expected to talk engagingly to one
another.) Fletcher had only contempt for people who ate "in the
same manner in which a man usually packs a trunk." Chewing
was a much more serious business than packing.

Fletcher used self-advertisement and propaganda to unusual
effect and soon became something of a celebrity. In 1903 he was
examined by doctors at Yale university, where Russell H.
Chittenden, a distinguished professor of physiological chemistry,
favorably received his regime of limited and exhaustive ingestion
combined with physical exercises. Although Chittenden was more
impressed by Fletcher's ability to survive on small amounts of
food than on his jaw movements, the message that gained cre-
dence was largely about chewing. Fletcher became known as the
"chew-chew man" by his detractors, but his fame went before
him. His 1913 magnum opus, *Fletcherism: What It Is,* was very
sympathetically reviewed by the *New York Times,* and gained him a
national reputation. Very soon Fletcher was holding forth in the

Ladies Home Journal, and his converts soon included a roster of famous names: Thomas Edison, John D. Rockefeller, Upton Sinclair, and Henry James. Another disciple, Dr. John Harvey Kellogg, argued that Fletcherizing saved money as well as improved health by cutting down on the consumption of meat and other "fancy foods."

Ultimately, the Great Masticator, as he came to be called, committed himself to almost ceaseless travel, signing up as a food economist in World War I in the conviction that better chewing would enable the Belgian people to surmount the hardships of inadequate clothing and food. He reportedly said that, "cut off from the world they have nothing else to do. Moreover, food is running short [in wartime Belgium] and can be made to last much longer by careful chewing." In the view of his obituary writers, Fletcher had taught the world how to chew, gluttony was no longer celebrated in America as it had been, and "slenderness began to gain some of the chic it would have among later generations."[14] Fletcher could hardly have understood how this cult of slimness would come to dominate a later generation.[15]

If the chewing gum story owes something to the American interest in chewing, it also owes a great deal to the developing taste for making and devouring confectionery. One person stands head and shoulders above the others in the burgeoning market for commercially produced candy that developed at the turn of the twentieth century. This was Milton S. Hershey, the inventor of the chocolate bar. Hershey's life has close parallels with chocolate manufacturers in England, notably the Quaker families of Cadbury and Fry. Like them he provided model employment conditions for the workforce and advocated social reform. Hershey was a Mennonite by birth, descended from Swiss immigrants and, at the age of eighteen, decided to go into business on his own, making candy. When he began, he tried to sell too many products and faced repeated commercial disasters and bankruptcies. Calling on friends to help put up the money for successive ventures, he eventually hit on the idea of covering his candies with chocolate after noticing, on a visit to England, that children there licked the chocolate coating off the sweets they consumed. By 1894 Hershey's Lancaster Caramel Company did more than a million dollars in business.

The secret of Hershey's success with the chocolate bar, like that of the early experiments with gum, was to constantly innovate, producing distinctive products, flavors, and wrapping. In a corner of his Lancaster Caramel Company, Hershey began experimenting with chocolate without caramels inside, leading to the introduction of Hershey's milk chocolate bar in 1900. This was an overnight success and, characteristically, Hershey invested part of his profits in an automobile, a novelty in itself, with a painted advertisement for his chocolate on the outside. At a much later date, chocolate bars, like chewing gum, became part of the American soldier's rations when Hershey was asked by the United States Army to make a bar of chocolate that would not melt in a soldier's pack. It had to be small, yet able to provide energy for a day of active service. The solution was the introduction of the Field Ration D chocolate bar. The *D* stood for "daily," and the Hershey factories were soon turning out more than half a million bars a day.[16]

Anyone Can Make Gum: Selling It Is the Problem

The pioneers of chewing gum, Thomas Adams and others, introduced chicle to the American diet, but it was left to another to make the marketing of gum into an art. This was William Wrigley

Jr., whose name was to become synonymous with chewing gum throughout the twentieth century. In the spring of 1891 Wrigley arrived in Chicago from Philadelphia. His father had manufactured scouring soap, peddling it from store to store. He then struck on the idea of offering storekeepers baking powder as a premium, an incentive to buy his soap. This proved to be so popular that Wrigley made baking powder his primary product, and he began offering two packets of chewing gum with each can of baking powder. Once again the premium eclipsed the original product, and Wrigley decided to enter the gum business on a serious footing.

Wrigley instructed the Zeno Gum Company to manufacture his product, requesting that they convert from paraffin gum to chicle. He noticed that women chewed more gum than men, and to exploit this market, he introduced Vassar, a brand named after the upmarket New York women's college. He then introduced a series of different branded gums in 1893, including what were to become Wrigley's trademarks: Juicy Fruit and Spearmint. At the time, the chewing gum field was highly competitive: There were at least a dozen companies that produced gum, six of which formed a "chewing gum trust," including the Adams company. What came to distinguish Wrigley from the rest was the originality and flair that he brought to advertising the product. "Anyone can make gum," he once said, "Selling it is the problem."[17]

When his products sold slowly, as Wrigley's Spearmint did at the beginning, his response was to undertake what would be called "pilot advertising" today. In 1906 he decided to advertise the gum on a modest scale in the three eastern cities of Buffalo, Rochester, and Syracuse. The results were so promising that he followed this with more intensive campaigns. He built huge advertising hoardings, and placards advertising his products appeared in streetcars and subways. He was one of the first businessmen to see the advantages of electric lighting and he put up electric signs; one in Manhattan's Times Square ran up an annual electric bill of more than $100,000. Later he constructed a line of 117 linked billboards advertising the merits of Wrigley's Spearmint, which lined the tracks of the railroad between Atlantic City and Trenton, New Jersey. It was the biggest advertising hoarding of its day.

Wrigley's other innovation was to exploit the fact that chewing gum constituted "something for nothing," and he began to send small samples of gum to millions of people. His aim was to make chewing gum indispensable by ensuring that it was taken everywhere and chewed at all times. In stores he ensured that small packets were placed next to the cash register, encouraging impulse buying by customers. As the United States entered an economic recession in 1907, Wrigley saw that people were less likely to forgo something cheap and enjoyable than other, more essential items. In fact, he stood logic on its head by investing in advertising throughout times of economic difficulty, and his annual sales soared despite the recession.

In addition to massive advertising through billboards and the dissemination of free gifts to millions of consumers, Wrigley also brought imagination and flair to the design of chewing gum wrappers. In 1915 he published a Mother Goose booklet and gave away 14 million copies. The rhymes in the booklet were rewritten to reflect the merits of Wrigley's gum: "Jack be nimble, Jack be quick, Jack run get your Wrigley stick!" The booklet not only refashioned traditional doggerel, it made explicit the connection between chewing gum and good health. (In this he was echoing Horace Fletcher.) A doctor urged readers to have plenty of chewing gum on hand to aid digestion. Other experts reminded the public that gum could calm nerves, relieve thirst, ease a sore throat, freshen breath, and aid appetite.

From 1915 to 1917 Wrigley sent free samples of gum to more than 8.5 million telephone subscribers. In another campaign he mailed two sticks of free gum to two-year-olds on their birthdays—more than three-quarters of a million children were targeted in this way. Using the power of radio, he later created the first singing commercials, or jingles, and even went on to sponsor a radio program, *The Lone Wolf,* for which six hundred thousand children signed up to join an "Indian tribe." These and similar campaigns eventually made Wrigley the largest purchaser of advertising in the United States, and this was at a time when public advertising was growing on an unprecedented scale.

Eventually Wrigley became a multimillionaire. He moved into organized sport, buying the Chicago Cubs baseball team in 1916, and the field on which they play is still named after him. He built an enormous aviary, housing six thousand birds, on the island of Catalina off the coast of California. An architect was commissioned to design his company skyscraper, which resembled a birthday cake with finger tracings in the icing. At the same time, by the standards of the day, he treated his workforce well. He provided free laundering of work clothes, free manicures for women workers, free life insurance, and a guaranteed annual wage. He was also the first employer in the United States to provide a two-day weekend for his employees. When he died in 1932, at the age of seventy, he was one of the ten wealthiest men in the United States. By establishing factories abroad, he stretched his empire to thirty-seven countries. His factories produced 280 million sticks of gum a week. Chewing gum had become part of the American way of life.

3

CHICLE AND SOCIAL REVOLUTION IN YUCATÁN

The invention of chicle-based chewing gum in the United States carried far-reaching implications for its geographical neighbor, Mexico. William Wrigley had convinced millions of Americans that they should buy his flavored gum. But at that very moment, the resin for chewing gum was being fought over in the jungles of the Yucatán Peninsula. In 1901 the chewing gum trust—made up of five of the six largest manufacturers in the United States—was established north of the border. Meanwhile, in Mexico, the production and sale of chicle on the part of rebel Mayan Indians or *caciques* was allowing them to buy arms to fight the Mexican government.[1] The Caste War of Yucatán, the name given to this armed conflict, has been described as the last great indigenous rebellion in the Americas. It was the largest and most protracted

Gulf
of
Mexico

Cabo Catoche

Motul
Mérida
Uman
Maxcanu
Halacho
Calkini
Tenebo
Campeche
Champoton

Izamal
Acanceh
Hocaba
Sotuta
Mani
Ticul
Tekax
Oxkutzcab
Puuc Hills
Bolonchen
Iturbide
Chenes
Muna

Tunkas
Tizimin
Espita
Tinum
Valladolid
Chichén itza
Chimimilá
Yaxcaba
Tixcacalcupul
Cocomes
Ichmul
Peto
Becanchen

Chancenote
Chemax
Tikuch
Xocen
Tepich
Tihosuco
Sacalaca
Tituc
Poliuc

Cozumel

Bahia de la
Ascención

Bahia de
Espiritu Santo

Parts said to be very thinly inhabited

Bacalar

Bahia de
Chetumal

Rio Hondo

Guatemala

Petén

British
Honduras

Belize

Gulf
of
Honduras

Map of Yucatán in 1847

of Mexico's rural rebellions, and it played a central role in the history of the country during the late nineteenth and twentieth centuries. But the legends and myths surrounding the Caste War were not confined to history. Today in Yucatán they still resonate for many of the Mayan people, and they have provided inspiration for modern popular dissent, much of it by ethnically Mayan groups, such as the Zapatistas in Chiapas, a neighboring province.

When Mexico became independent, the principal beneficiaries were the white Creole elite. The Spanish governor of Yucatán resigned without a fight, and the peninsula joined the Mexican Union. Not surprisingly, the majority of the indigenous population also entertained hopes of a much better future. Fewer than 300,000 Mayas had survived the brutality of the Spanish Conquest, but in the succeeding three centuries their numbers had gradually begun to climb. The total population of the Yucatán Peninsula, which was at its lowest in 1700, at about 130,000, had risen to more than half a million by 1845, two years before the outbreak of the Caste War.

The Caste War of Yucatán

To fully appreciate the importance of these events and their contribution to the chewing gum story, we need to follow the narrative back to 1821, when Mexico gained independence from Spain. The Yucatán had always retained a degree of independence from the rest of Mexico, partly because of its geographical position. Indeed, until independence in 1821, Spain had administered it separately from the rest of Mexico. After independence the historical trajectory of the peninsula departed ever more radically from that of the new Mexican republic. In 1839 Santiago Imam launched a revolt that formally separated Yucatán from the rest of Mexico, but this brief flirtation with independence did not succeed for more than a few months. He promised the abolition of taxes on the Maya, and the expectation of these reforms—some of which were incorporated into the 1841 constitution—ignited high expectations among the Mayan peasantry. They can be seen, with hindsight, as prompting millenarian instincts, which were channeled in the direction of Mayan independence and cultural autarky during the subsequent century.

Most of the indigenous Mayan farmers were dependent on corn as their food staple, and their cornfields (the *milpa*) were the center of their ceremonial life. After 1825 this subsistence economy was increasingly placed in jeopardy by the expansion of a new cash crop, sugarcane, which was being grown on large estates. Sugarcane required high-quality land, but the financial returns on investment were extremely profitable, and landlords began to employ increasing numbers of dispossessed and marginal *campesinos*. Many of the Mayan peasants, already subjected to onerous taxes and labor obligations by the whites (*dzul*), fled into the jungle to the east of the peninsula, today's province of Quintana Roo. In the forests of the east and south, Mayan resentment at the trick played on them by the dominant white population was nurtured and grew. To most of the peasant farmers, independence from Spain had opened possibilities of easing their subjugation and granting them rights as free and equal citizens. Their unease grew into unrest and eventually, in the town of Tepich just south of Valladolid, their rebellion started.

The white authorities were alerted to an impending rebellion by the movement of population within the territory between

Valladolid, the center of white supremacy, and Tepich and Tihosuco, to the south. The Indians were anticipating conflict by leaving the colonial towns where they were subjects and occupying the dense forests where they could disappear from view. A movement of organized resistance was born. Unsuccessful attempts were made to detain two of the movement's leaders, Jacinto Pat and Cecilio Chi. However, a third Mayan leader, Manuel Antonio Ay, was arrested in possession of a letter giving information about an indigenous uprising. On July 26, 1847, Ay was shot in Valladolid, in front of a large gathering of Mayan onlookers.

The assassination of Ay was a miscalculation of historic proportions for several reasons. First, it set a new precedent, since Ay was the first political prisoner for some years to be shot while detained by the white authorities. Second, it sent a message to the other leaders, notably Jacinto Pat and Cecilio Chi, that in the future they could place no trust in the whites and should remain out of reach in the forest. Third, the execution drove a wedge between the Mayan population and the Yucatecan whites (the federalists), who were pressing for independence from the rest of Mexico. Immediately after the event, Cecilio Chi led his men into the village of Tepich, where they massacred twenty white families. This, in turn, provoked reprisals and led to a state of alert on both sides of the conflict.

The immediate political result was the leading Yucatecan whites' rescinding the very limited concessions they had made to the Mayan population in the 1841 constitution and introducing conscription for the white population so that they could defend themselves. On the large sugar estates the Indian population was forcibly disarmed, and those who resisted fought against the

Tihosuco Church—cradle of the
Caste War

Maya who remained loyal to their Yucatecan landlords. At the same time the Mayan rebel leaders regrouped and met at the village of Culumpich, where they determined to rid themselves of the whites who had long oppressed them.

During the early stages of the Caste War, the Mayan armies were very successful. By the end of March 1848, most of the east of the peninsula was in Indian hands, and a force of fifteen thousand men had taken the strategically vital city of Valladolid. The fugitive white population that left the city of Valladolid for Merida, to the west, was massacred on the road. In a letter to the governor of Yucatán, the Mayan rebels pointed out that the whites had initiated the atrocities, and they were left with no alternative but to defend themselves from the cycle of oppression. In April, Jacinto Pat agreed to meet with the whites in the village of Tzucacab, where he laid out the conditions under which the rebels could be persuaded to lay down their arms.

There were eight demands that the whites needed to meet. First, the landlord's right to the personal labor of the subject Indian had to be abolished. Second, the Mayan population should possess the same rights governing baptism and marriage as the white population. Third, they should have guaranteed access to common lands, especially forests, without interference from the whites. Fourth, the Mayan population, which had been forced into servile indebtedness to whites, would have those debts rescinded. Fifth, they sought the investiture of a new governor who was sympathetic to them (Don Miguel Barbachano), and sixth, Jacinto Pat would be accepted as the acknowledged leader of the Maya. Seventh, the rebels demanded the return of the 2,500 rifles that had been confiscated. Finally, all taxes on the distilling of liquor from sugarcane would be abolished.

The whites accepted these reforms, which constituted little more than the restitution to the Mayans of rights that had been recently abrogated. However, one of the rebel leaders, Cecilio Chi, refused to accept the agreement entered into at Tzucacab and argued that the only viable outcome was for the whites to relinquish their control completely or to be extinguished. The war consequently continued, and when the Mayan forces had conquered three-quarters of the peninsula, the whites retreated to the only two cities that offered them any protection: Merida and Campeche.

At this point the war took a surprising turn. Having arrived within thirty kilometers of Merida, the Mayan armies suddenly turned around and left the field of battle. The explanation normally provided is that the Maya returned in June to their cornfields in the west to sow the next season's crop. Since they were peasant farmers rather than soldiers, their first priority was their own subsistence, and this could only be guaranteed through the cultivation of the *milpa*. However, it also has been suggested that the Mayan forces had no territorial ambitions as such, and their return to the fields represented a logical step for an army of resistance rather than of conquest.[2]

Whatever the reasons for the retreat, those who remained to fight the whites were easily beaten back until the Mayan armies had retreated into the forest vastness to the east. By the end of 1848, whites again ruled all the major centers of population and Cecilio Chi had been assassinated. The retreating Maya sowed their corn in the jungle to the east and south of the peninsula, where they remained in open rebellion under new leadership. They were a dispirited army, which, by 1850, had apparently lost the battle for possession of Yucatán.

At this point something altogether surprising happened, although it was consistent with what we know about revivalism among subjugated peoples.[3] Jose Maria Barrera, the mixed-race leader of a small troop of Mayan rebels, strayed with his band into an uninhabited section of forest, to a *cenote* (or sinkhole in the limestone plateau) used only by wandering tribesmen.[4] One of the group was Juan de la Cruz Puc, who had been trained to read, write, and lead religious ceremonies. He was from Xocen, a village near Valladolid that the Maya believed (and many still believe) was the center of the world. Growing from the mouth of the cave, watered by the spirit of the *cenote*, was an old mahogany tree. According to Mayan teaching, this suggested that the underworld was not far away. This was hidden territory, unknown to the *dzul* but representative of the core beliefs about nature and the gods in the Mayan cosmology. On this tree Juan found a small cross carved into the mahogany trunk, and the significance of the find was not lost on the group. The emblematic elements in Mayan cosmology were all present: the cave, the *cenote*, the tree, and the cross.

Juan recognized the cross as the unmovable Santissima Cruz Tan from his village of Xocen. It had traveled underground, as things do, along the subterranean water tunnels, and appeared to him one hundred kilometers to the south. The cross became a *santo*, a saint, able to communicate with the most powerful figure in the Christian world, Jesus Christ. This transfiguration, as Nelson Reed reminds us, "may be described as a religious vision in which a member of a defeated remnant took on the persona of the most powerful figure known to his world."[5]

The communication took place within Juan's head, for he could hear the cross speaking, but for the messages to be intelligible to others, it was necessary for the "Talking Cross" to have another conduit for expression. Juan found that one of his companions, Manuel Nauat, was able to provide a voice for the cross; he was able to project the words as if they were spoken by the cross itself, as a ventriloquist does. Although, from the perspective of the twenty-first century, this technique (and later ones) was clearly a deliberate manipulation; it also could be seen as an effective way of spreading the idea of hope among the Mayan population. The message spread, slowly at first and then with speed, especially through written commandments from the cross: The whites would never succeed; victory would lie with the followers of the Mayan cross.

In the early hours of January 4, 1851, the Mayan rebels stormed the nearest Yucatecan army base, suffering heavy losses. The whites took many prisoners and determined to end the rebellion by capturing the cross itself and destroying it. But those who were taken prisoner by the whites found new strength from their insurrection—they became the *Cruzoob*. The cross carved in the tree had become three crosses, and they had ceased to be merely carvings; they had become objects in their own right, evidence of profound truths. They said the hour had struck when the Mayan peasants would again govern their own land. The three crosses were dressed in miniature *huipil* (Mayan smocks) and skirts. They were decorated, as were all Mayan crosses, with bright ribbons. The new cult became known as "Balam Na, Chan Santa Cruz," and the little huts in the forest soon formed a new town, the epicenter of a new kernel of resistance. It was a rallying point for the rebel Maya, the base from which they fought a guerrilla war. In the town, a permanent armed guard was soon established to protect the temple they had built and dedicated to the cross.

Every time the whites attacked the citadel of Mayan rebellion they found it either well defended or strategically abandoned. In effect, it was virtually invulnerable. Between 1854 and 1855 the army of Yucatán tried repeatedly to pacify the Maya of the Talking Cross. But the rebel Maya always struck back. On one occasion they poisoned the drinking water of their white adversaries with the polluted clothes of cholera victims. The forest to the east and south of Yucatán represented an apparently impenetrable hell, and even some of the Yucatecan soldiers came to believe in the power of the cross, and they left the field of combat. Probably half of those who fought on both sides were killed in action, and many more died of cholera or from disabling wounds. It was a war of attrition that the whites would never win. Nevertheless, at this point "it was decided that the rebellion called the Caste War had come to an end. There had been no final victory, and there would be fighting for the rest of the century. . . . Of all the native revolts in America since the Arawaks used their wooden spears against the sailors of Columbus, this one alone had succeeded."[6] The whites had declared, unilaterally, that the Caste War had ended. For the rebel Maya, however, it would not end until they were able to practice their own religious rights in their own sacred territory.

Who Won the Caste War?

When military victory was within their grasp, many of the Mayan warriors, who were first and foremost peasant farmers, left the military front to return to their homes to plant the sacred corn. A professional army is unlikely to have behaved in this way, but it must be remembered that the Maya saw themselves not as conquerors with imperial ambitions but as a people who merely wanted to be left in peace, to plant their *milpa*. The Caste War signaled the impatience of the Mayan people, who had never sought victory against the whites. They sought merely the restitution of their traditional rights and freedom from the onerous obligations opened up by the transition to agrarian capitalism. (We might also note that similar forces and contradictions led Emiliano Zapata into armed opposition to landowners in Mexico after 1910, the beginning of another indigenous revolution in Mexico.) From passive resistance to onerous labor obligations, the Mayan rebellion spread to armed conflict against the whites and, ultimately, to the creation of a religious and spiritual alternative, in the form of a millenarian cult: the Talking Cross.

As Nelson Reed, the Caste War's most original interpreter, reminds us, at the time of Mexican independence from Spain in 1821, more people meant the need for more food, and this in turn provoked an intense struggle for land.[7] The Maya were taxed and exploited to fill the coffers of the Catholic Church and the Spanish Crown, but few benefits from colonial rule were visible to them. In 1814, Spain briefly passed a corpus of revolutionary laws, which applied to her empire as well as to the Spanish peninsula. These laws were briefly introduced in Mexico. They not only sought to guarantee the freedom of the press, local elections, and the abolition of forced labor, but also exacted tribute to the Spanish Crown as well as church taxes. Their importance was not lost on the Mayan Indians of the Yucatán. They hoped that an independent Mexico would enact them and bring freedom to an oppressed people.

Church of the Talking Cross today in Quintana Roo

This was not to be. Not only were civil liberties and freedom from excessive taxation denied to the Maya, but also their own land was put in jeopardy by the expansion of new commercial agricultural enterprises—particularly henequen (or sisal)—that began in the 1830s. After independence, the marked differences between the whites and the Maya did not diminish; in fact, they often increased. The Maya were increasingly confined to their communities, and political control, previously exercised by the colonial state, was now in the hands of an increasingly intolerant white elite.

Finally, the event that held most importance for the future of the Mayan rebels was unusual, to say the least. It marked the collision of premodernity in the form of the Talking Cross, and the inexorable march of modern history. Although demoralized, the rebel Maya sought comfort and deliverance in the form of an apparition, which became the medium through which God talked to them, his chosen people, and advised them on their military conduct. The location of this event became transformed into a sacred site. Although pushed back into the dense forest, the Maya had not been defeated, but were subjected to what we would today call a standoff. The Mexican authorities left tacit control in the hands of the Mayan chieftain and were only represented by isolated outposts that were difficult to protect.

The last half of the nineteenth century marked a prolonged and bloody campaign of resistance and counterinsurgency. In 1858 the Mayan rebels massacred the inhabitants of the fortress of Bacalar, an outpost of white authority in an area of strong Mayan opposition in southern Quintana Roo. The rebel Mayan army took the fortress and held it for several years against white opposition. The Belizeans of British Honduras (today's Belize), to the south, were supplying the rebel Maya with arms and, in an effort to curb this supply, a customs post was established at the mouth of the Rio Hondo in 1898, where the town of Payo Obispo (today's Chetumal) was founded. The prospect of continued Mayan resistance led the Mexican army to try to isolate the rebellion from the south. Payo Obispo served as a base for the recolonization and pacification of the Maya in the south, on the border with British Honduras.

However, farther to the north, the Mexican general Ignacio Bravo undertook a much more ruthless suppression of dissent, which began with the capture of the rebel Mayan capital in 1901. On May 4, 1901, General Bravo led his men into the heartland of indigenous opposition, capturing "Noh Cah Balam Na Santa Cruz" (literally, "the place of the Talking Cross"), the capital of the rebellious Maya and the center of the chicle-producing zone on the Yucatán Peninsula. This was a poignant defeat of a people who had demonstrated extraordinary religious, political, and economic independence from the Mexican state for more than half a century.[8]

That the rebel Maya were able to successfully resist cultural and political domination, even after the Mexican army's control was reestablished in 1901, is largely explained by the role chicle came to play in the forest economy of the region. During the last few decades of the nineteenth century, the rebel Maya were forced back into the jungle, but they were able to obtain arms by selling the chicle resin that was produced from their forests. The sale of this gum was controlled by a Mayan *cacique*, General May, who used his political influence and military power to provide protection for both the men who tapped the gum and the contractors who bought it from them.[9]

The large gum manufacturers in the United States, notably William Wrigley, were dependent on General May for the transport of their supplies, and the Mayan armies were able to buy weapons from the proceeds of these sales. Much of the gum was sold illegally through British Honduras. One of the most important motives for seeking this solution was to avoid paying excise duty to the Mexican authorities. These political and economic ambitions, at the margin of legality and deeply resented by the Mexican state, served to cement links between British banks—particularly the Bank of London and Mexico—American manufacturers, and the Mayan insurgents.[10] For the essentially autonomous rebel Maya, the apogee of their independence from Mexico occurred at the close of the nineteenth century, when they took the step of petitioning Queen Victoria, unsuccessfully, to become part of the British Empire.[11]

From the perspective of London, the insurgent Mayan army in Yucatán must have seemed a ragbag, and their land hardly a potential jewel in the British Crown, but the appetite for chewing gum in the United States helped to keep their cause alive. Wrigley exerted the power of the American dollar, entering into contracts with Mayan rebels, with whom the Mexican state still regarded as bitter enemies and refused to meet except as vanquished "Indians." Paradoxically, and unwittingly then, the consumers of chewing gum in the United States were keeping alive the beliefs and convictions of a people they would never meet, whose rebel army patrolled the thatched-roofed barracks of villages deep in the Yucatán forest. There is perhaps a dual irony here: Not only was the U.S. citizen unknowingly supporting an indigenous rebellion by chewing gum, but did so at a time when the Native American population of the United States was being politically and culturally repressed.

Chicle and the Rebel Maya

It has been estimated that the population of independent Cruzoob Maya was about eighty-five thousand in 1850. During the next fifty years it declined, with some people moving into British Honduras to the south, others into the "pacified areas" of Yucatán to the north and west. In most of the peninsula of Yucatán, a new activity, the production of henequen (or sisal) from the leaves of a local agave, brought prosperity to landlords and merchants. Technical developments, such as the development of steam-powered decorticating mills, enabled the coarse fiber to be removed from the fleshy leaves of the plant. In the days before artificial fibers, sisal had a number of essential uses, such as for making ropes, carpets, and rugs. The technological breakthrough, represented by henequen production, and the economic prosperity it brought to Yucatán, was similar to the role of the cotton gin in the southern United States. Soon the streets of Merida were lined with carriages and exquisite *fin-de-siècle* mansions, like the Paseo de Montejo, which was modeled on the Champs-Élysées in Paris. In fact, in terms of culture and taste, Merida was closer to Paris and London in some respects than to Mexico City. The wealth brought by the market for henequen in Europe and North America had served to develop and consolidate a new cosmopolitan spirit.

To the east and south, the people of the Talking Cross still controlled the forest and, most important, its resources. The legacy of the Caste War, and the geopolitics of the region, had created conditions that were very favorable for foreign commercial access to the region's resources.[12] Already, financial interests based in London had established a flourishing logwood and cabinet-wood business in Belize (British Honduras). By the mid-nineteenth century, logwood extraction had penetrated farther up the Caribbean coast of Quintana Roo. After logwood declined the trade in mahogany and other valuable hardwoods expanded, and incursions farther into the forest, on the part of entrepreneurs and contractors, became common.

The military conflicts in Yucatán, and the increasing involvement of the authorities in British Honduras to the south, provided both commercial and diplomatic possibilities for foreign capital. Suddenly the forests of the Yucatán Peninsula were no longer just a source of valuable timber extraction—they became the seat of a new commercial activity that fed the tastes of consumers on the eastern seaboard of the United States. By the 1890s chicle was in demand in the United States.

The scale of the early chicle trade can be inferred from the annual *Bluebooks*, which summarized the economic activities of British Honduras in this period. They show a gradual increase in the importance of chicle, and other forest products, from slightly more than 60 percent of export value in 1886, to about 80 percent by 1900. A little less than half of these exports were probably sourced from the Yucatán. Within ten years the official value of chicle exports rose by 72 percent. As the forest resources of British Honduras gradually became depleted, further incursions were made into Quintana Roo and the territory controlled by the Cruzoob. In fact, as most trade with what was formally Mexican territory was forbidden or discouraged, the statistics that exist almost certainly underestimate the importance of sourcing from Quintana Roo.

These figures also give us some idea of the importance of foreign capital for the region in this period. Access to Quintana Roo's products was possible because, for half a century, the British had

Blocks of chicle *(marquetas)* awaiting collection

provided support to the rebel Maya, sometimes tacitly, less often overtly. At the same time, London was anxious to maintain reasonably good relations with Mexico City, precisely to gain access to southern Quintana Roo for its own commerce. British investment in Mexico had a long history, dating back to the early postindependence period. By the mid-1880s, Mexico's external debt to Britain was £23 million, which suggests very high levels of British investment. And it was actively encouraged by the government of the dictator Porfirio Diaz.[13]

In the absence of Mexican capital every effort was made to develop the region with whatever foreign capital was available.[12] In 1892 London companies established the Mexican Exploration Company to extract forest products in coastal areas near the Bay of Chetumal. This company was later declared bankrupt, but its concessions were taken over by another company, based in Belize, in 1896. In the same year yet another enterprise, the East Coast of Yucatán Colonization Company, was formed in Mexico City but was financed by the Bank of London and Mexico. This company took over an earlier concession, which gave it access to nearly three-quarters of a million hectares of forest.[13]

These huge concessions, negotiated with British and other foreign companies, gave them access to forest resources that were effectively barred to the Mexican authorities before 1901. They positioned British capital to exploit almost the entire eastern seaboard of the Yucatán Peninsula. In 1893 the Mexican and British governments had entered into a settlement known as the Mariscal–St. John Treaty, which made the Rio Hondo the southern border of Mexican territory with British Honduras. Via this strategic river system, the British now had greater access to Quintana Roo, and it consolidated their position with the Cruzoob. At the same time, it might also have undermined the rebel Maya in the longer term, by introducing commercial relations. The Maya became increasingly drawn into this web, which dramatically transformed the culture as well as the economy of the region.

As early as 1894 the government of Diaz had passed comprehensive legislation regulating the exploitation of forest products and lands, which had increasingly fallen under the control of foreign commercial interests. This legislation would become the basis for future concessions to foreigners, for which the Mexican federal government sought adequate compensation. The exploitation of Quintana Roo's forests had been stimulated by the growth of trade of chicle with the United States. The rebel Maya had derived benefits from this trade, and the Mexican government sought, through regulating trade, to cut off supplies of cash and arms to the Mayan rebels.

The Mexican government initiated its military campaign from the sea, in an effort to strengthen communication between the coast of Quintana Roo and the rest of the country. A small naval force was sent to Cozumel and the Bay of Chetumal to the south to provide bridgeheads for later expansion. As a condition of signing the Mariscal–St. John Treaty, the British government had agreed to prevent arms from reaching the Cruzoob through Belize, and this new naval force helped to ensure compliance. This campaign began in 1898 with the patrolling of the Rio Hondo boundary by an armed naval customs vessel. The principal attack on the rebel Maya, however, would be overland from the west, using the town of Peto as the main point of departure.

In the short period between December 1899 and May 1901, the army of General Bravo gradually opened up the territory of Quintana Roo controlled by the Cruzoob. In effect, the federal army's work consisted of protecting the work gangs, which were constructing the rail link to Peto. Their superior ammunitions meant that they were able to defeat the Mayan forces in a series of skirmishes that were understood at the time as battles of vital national importance. The losses were not great on either side, but General Bravo made it his business to keep the authorities informed of his progress, cabling both Merida and Mexico City at different stages of the conflict. These were strategic victories rather than heroic military adventures, and more men were lost through fever, dysentery, and malnutrition than through battles. But the objective was finally achieved.

The government's campaign highlighted the fact that the Cruzoob were unable to prevent a serious military attack on their territory. The steam-driven railway, protected by guns and motivated by commercial gain, proved to be invincible. As one commentator put it, in an eloquent phrase, "The spikes of the commercial development . . . were being driven into the heart of the *Cruzoob* territory."[14] The Maya's response following military defeat, however, did not finally put an end to their cultural resistance. It merely displaced it geographically, and the rebels guarded their crosses with increased care.[15]

The Rebel Maya and the Rise of General May

The Cruzoob were driven from their capital Noh Cah Balam Na Santa Cruz on the morning of May 4, 1901.[16] They did not disappear, however; they merely retreated farther into the forest. General Bravo had medals cut in his honor, and the march of progress continued apace. Soon the telegraph wires, which had spread farther with the Mexican army's advance, sent the message out from the coast: The area had been reconquered and was now safe again for the whites.

Defeat for the rebel Maya was extremely painful. Many of them fled farther into the forest; for many there was nowhere else to go. Others crossed over into British Honduras, joined their compatriots there, and went on to found a refuge in the forests of northern Guatemala. Others stayed put and were eventually discovered by the invading Mexican army. Their military tactics were useless against superior arms—they could fight with machetes against single-shot rifles but not against machine guns. Most of them were rounded up over the next few years and were either killed on the spot or marched off to Peto, and from there they were handed over to landowners to use as they wished. The "stated purpose was to free them from their savage habits, to open for them a civilized horizon."[17]

The Mexican forces of occupation then began to construct means of communication between Chan Santa Cruz (renamed Santa Cruz de Bravo after the Mexican general who took the capital) and the coast. President Diaz decreed from Mexico City that the new territory should be called the Federal Territory of Quintana Roo, named for a hero of the independence struggle. Yucatecs did not like it, since they considered the territory their backyard, and they criticized the Mexican authorities for taking it from their jurisdiction. At the same time a smaller number of Yucatecs benefited from the new status, having been given both vast concessions to exploit the forests and a free hand with the natives.[18]

Access to the forests was the first priority of the new regime, for whom the conquest had been little more than a construction project. It was decided that, since Santa Cruz was only thirty-six miles from the sea, across mangrove swamps, versus the ninety miles to the railhead at Peto, it would be better to build the railroad to the sea. A new site was chosen as a port, called Vigia Chico, which became the local entrepôt for lucrative forest products. In the first decade of the twentieth century, Vigia Chico was a hated place, consisting of several whorehouses, a barracks, a hotel with a veranda, and an enormous pier. Indicative of the quality of life in Vigia Chico at the time is the suggestion that the interior design of some of the buildings came to reflect the lifestyles of most of the inhabitants in unorthodox ways. As Reed comments, "The presence of glass floors in several of the buildings, [were] made by pushing rum bottles upside down into the sand."[19]

However, the important thing was that if a railroad was completed to the coast, then a secure way of getting chicle and hardwoods to the market had been found. So, under the new Mexican commanding officer, General Vega, a railroad was built, although at great human cost. Platforms, drawn by mules and steam locomotives, were hauled along narrow-gauge tracks from the port through jungle and swamps. Nobody who possessed any civil liberties could be induced to join the labor force for the purpose, so the contractors used political prisoners and convicts. If they tried to escape, they were shot. At the halfway point, a guards' barrack was added to the installations, since recalcitrant Maya had been taking potshots at members of the garrison. An army marksman armed with telescopic sights discovered them and managed to shoot the enemy with his Mauser field gun. The tree from which the Mayan rebels were dispatched was called *El Indio Triste* (the sad Indian).[20]

Among the rebel Maya who took aim at the garrison and the workers on the railroad was a young man called Francisco May. He would play an important role during the next thirty years.

May was the son of Damaso May and Maria Pech, but his father died when he was two years old, and his mother married another local Mayan leader, Felipe Yama. Local accounts suggest that his stepfather inspired the bravery May displayed in the charges he led against the tractor that transported chicle to the coast. It marked him out as a potential leader and accelerated his rise within the Mayan rebel army.

It was May who, as a leader, or *cacique,* was to act as a conduit between those who had been given concessions to exploit the forest and the Mexican government. Taking the military rank of general within the Mayan rebel army, by a curious turn of fate General May assumed power over the remaining Cruzoob just as Mexico plunged into domestic turmoil. In 1910 the Mexican Revolution began, although it was two years before it arrived in Quintana Roo. A new, revolutionary general, Manuel Sanchez Rivera, arrived in Santa Cruz from Vigia Chico with fifty soldiers. His mission was to explain to the aged General Bravo that his control was at an end. A banquet was served in the center of the rebel heartland, Chan Santa Cruz (de Bravo), under the orange trees. The political prisoners were freed and given passports, travel vouchers, and money. General Bravo fled to Vigia Chico and on to Mexico City, only concerned with saving his life.

The revolutionary forces tried to make contact with the Cruzoob by hanging messages in bottles on trees, but to no avail. The mistrust between the Maya and the whites, even revolutionary whites, was too great to end overnight. Within two years, however, a new socialist governor of Yucatán ordered that the capital of Quintana Roo would be moved south to Chetumal, and the Indians were given definitive control of their own sacred place, Noh, Cah Balam Nah Santa Cruz, in 1917. Having been liberated by the Mexican Revolution, the remaining Mayan rebels were afflicted with smallpox, halving the population to about five thousand. However, the Talking Cross had survived, hidden from the excesses of General Bravo's army of occupation, which had desecrated the temple, the Balam N'a.

Another survivor of both the war and smallpox was General Francisco May, and, as the commander of the rebel Mayan forces south of the Yucatán Peninsula, it was he who benefited from the boom in chicle production.

The Chicle Concessionaries

The taste for chewing gum, nurtured by consumers in the United States and funded partly by British capital in Mexico, led an army of new adventurers deep into the forests of Quintana Roo. Many of the chicleros who arrived in the first decade of the twentieth century were from other Mexican states, such as Veracruz, Chiapas, and Yucatán as well as Belize. By 1915 more than three-quarters of the chicle imported into the United States came from Mexico. The connection between the Caste War and the chicle story rests on the historical dependency of American gum manufacturers on supplies from land that was mostly controlled by the rebel Mayan army. The Maya saw chicle as an opportunity to finance their rebellion, and the chicle manufacturers, in turn, turned to the rebel Maya to guarantee their forest concessions and, if necessary, to provide armed protection.

The Maya often stole the mules and supplies from the adventurers who entered their forests, but most did not become chicleros until the 1920s. Although they had effective control of their forests from 1914, harvesting chicle was not their primary economic activity. Until World War I the harvesting of chicle had been little more than a new economic incursion, like many earlier examples of outside intervention in their forests. The Caste War had reached an impasse, if not a conclusion. Now, the expansion of chicle offered the Maya hope of a renewed source of finance for their attempt at autarky.

By 1917 the situation began to change dramatically. The first large-scale chicle contractor was a Cuban called Julio Martin, who made an agreement with General May giving Martin the right to exploit a concession on territory controlled by the Maya. After Martin other concessionaries arrived, including Wrigley's from the United States, La Compania Mexicana from Mexico, and an influential intermediary, Mr. Turton, based in Belize. "Casa Martin" began to establish camps and collection points near Chan Santa Cruz, while in the north an important collection center was established inland from Puerto Morelos. Now the rebel Maya were poised to take advantage of the new commercial opportunities offered by chicle, and to do so without any significant concessions to the Mexican revolutionary government, which itself was largely distracted by events elsewhere in the republic.

By the boom years of the late 1920s, there were more than fifteen hundred chicleros working at this center—Central Vallarta—during the harvest season, from September to January. From Santa Cruz in the south, the chicle was transported to the port of Vigia Chico. The tractors used for transporting the gum carried 4,600 kilos of chicle a day, 27,000 kilos a week. It soon became apparent that only a small proportion of the forest's potential could be exploited by outside contractors because of difficulty in recruiting labor, fever, and the constant attacks from groups of Maya. Armed guards were needed to protect the encampments of the first chicleros. The chewing gum manufacturers and the contractors who employed chicleros, both American and Mexican in southern Quintana Roo, looked to General May as their only source of protection. The Mexican government was impotent and had effectively ceded control to May and his followers in the region. But May had proved that a poacher could successfully turn into a gamekeeper and by 1917 had discovered the potential offered by chicle.

The platform and tractor for transporting the chicle belonged to General May, but the railway line was owned by a chicle contractor called Miguel Angel Ramoneda. In 1924 Ramoneda had received a concession from the Mexican Ministry of War and Sea Defenses, much to May's disapproval, since his men had built the line.

The Mexican Federal Department of Forestry authorized concessions for the harvest of chicle from both Mexicans and foreigners, but, importantly, nobody was allowed to take out chicle without it passing through the hands of General May. May acted as the intermediary who controlled the local trade in chicle. He provided contractors with military protection in exchange for goods and a share in the chicle harvest, which he later sold to the large international companies.[21]

In 1918 the Mexican president Carranza, aware of the potential riches of the region and the political sensitivities, invited May to Mexico City. May went by steamer to Vera Cruz and then on to the capital. There he met Venustiano Carranza, a tall man with a white beard, who was quite prepared to act the part of a "great white Mexican father" (*nohoch tata waach*) to the Mayan warrior. May swore on oath that he would pacify his area, and he was formally commissioned a general in the Mexican army, complete with gold-braided uniform and ceremonial sword. It might have appeared that the Mexican authorities had duped May, but, in a sense, the reverse was true. He had confirmation of his authority over twenty thousand hectares of forest, without paying tax, and he acquired the right to use the railroad system.[22]

The regime instituted by General May had all the hallmarks of a Mexican *caciquismo*. Although virtually illiterate, May proved an effective businessman with an astuteness that he concealed behind an apparently simple exterior. It seems likely that he took great pains to disguise his real understanding of events and their implications for the rebel Maya who he commanded. May exercised his authority through his command of a military force. He had twenty-five personal guards, and he took overall command of the local population. People within his jurisdiction received lashes with a whip for any perceived wrongdoing and were forced to enter the church and promise, after praying in Maya, not to reoffend. Foreigners living in the area were subjected to similar treatment, and sexual abuses and marital infidelity by women were very severely sanctioned. May's was a highly autocratic and intolerant fiefdom, while at the same time demonstrating the capacity of the Maya to exercise their own civil power.

May's tough regime also had a more progressive side, however. When the socialist Felipe Carrillo Puerto was appointed governor of Yucatán, there was a brief period of cooperation with May. This ended abruptly with Carrillo Puerto's assassination in 1924. President Carranza had already promised May that schools would be built in Quintana Roo, on May's insistence, and schools were built at Chancah, Dzula, Santa Maria, and Chumpon. In 1922, with Carrillo Puerto's support, May established the first Mayan chicle cooperatives in the state, a move that was to prove the harbinger of a new social institution.

Nevertheless, the ruthless maintenance of his authority ultimately undermined May's position in the eyes of the Mexican federal government. Several incidents contributed to his eventual demise. A chiclero, Santiago Borges, was accused of refusing to go to work in the forest, although he and his companions claimed that the rains prevented them from working. Borges was condemned to twenty-five strokes by May, and a misunderstanding led to this punishment being increased to fifty strokes. Borges later reported these abuses to a newspaper published in Cozumel, and the publicity surrounding the incident soon extended to Mexico City.[23]

In an historic pact in 1929, the federal authorities dictated new terms of compliance to May. He was deprived of the power to punish offenders within his jurisdiction, and civil registration and tax collection was handed over to the federal government. The Maya also were instructed not to fly the British Union Jack flag in their villages. Not for the first time they were told that henceforth they were a part of the Mexican federal state. On June 2, 1929, General Siurrob, of the Mexican army, entered Chan Santa Cruz and, after a great fiesta, he and May publicly embraced. This represented the effective transfer of power from the fiefdom of a traditional *cacique* to the Mexican state.[24]

Perhaps the most important factor in the downfall of General May was the fall in the world price for chicle, a consequence of the "Great Crash," but for which he was blamed personally. Previously, there had been limited opposition from within the ranks of the Maya, who objected to the iron hand of his rule. In Chumpon, to the north of the area he controlled, the production of chicle was controlled by Mayan leaders other than General May, and other independent contractors also penetrated the area. The Bank of London and Mexico directly controlled the zone of Kantunilkin. So, although General May was the leading Mayan chief in the south, in other chicle-producing areas the control exercised on concessionaries was much looser.

Much of the chicle from the territory of General May found its way southward, as we have seen, into British Honduras. To the north of May's fiefdom the story was different—chicle found its way from the coast around Tulum to the offshore island of Cozumel. Around Tulum, for almost twenty years production had been in the hands of the Cue brothers from Merida. Chicle from these areas was exported northward by rail to Puerto Morelos, which was only forty kilometers from Santa Maria, their estate. From Puerto Morelos the chicle went in small boats to Cozumel, where the vessels owned by the big chewing gum companies came to collect it. Cozumel became, in fact, the leading entrepôt for the chicle trade in the region for many of the most important concessionaries. From Puerto Morelos cargo was also sent to Progreso, on the Gulf coast of Yucatán. An air service was even planned in 1929, at the height of the boom and before the crash, linking Yucatán with Cuba.

The 1920s saw the explosion of chicle production in Quintana Roo, with more than six thousand chicleros arriving from other parts of Mexico and Central America. During the period in which May dominated the southern zone, each chiclero earned about fourteen pesos for each *quintal*, equivalent to forty-six kilos, of chicle. When food and other essential costs were taken into account, this left the average chiclero with about fifteen pesos (about one U.S. dollar) a day.

During most of the 1920s, chicleros earned about 300 pesos a month, but by 1929 this had risen to 1,800 pesos. This was the period of relative affluence, when chicleros came down from the forests and spent their surpluses on jewelry in the shops of Valladolid. While they were in the forests chicleros were able to buy items that had not been available twenty years earlier: whiskey and cigarettes as well as weapons. Indeed, the effect of alcoholism among forest workers was such that, in 1929, echoing the United States, prohibition was declared in the territory, although this did little to prevent contraband liquor from arriving from Belize.

In 1923 the first factories for manufacturing chewing gum were established in Mexico. Two years later more than 1 million kilos of chicle was exported officially. By 1929 production reached its peak for the decade: 2,400,000 kilos. The 1930s proved to be a decade of relative prosperity for most chicleros, despite the fall in price on the world market, since the workers were better organized and won more support from the government.[25] In 1933 production had dropped dramatically—to less than 700,000 kilos, and only half that figure in the following year. However, this drop did not immediately affect livelihoods adversely, since a great deal of the trade via Belize was still illegal and much of the production was not accounted for in official Mexican statistics. Most of the profits from the chicle trade went to General May and the contractors with whom he worked; in the areas he commanded in the south of the territory, he played a key part in "orchestrating the conversion of the Cruzoob local economy from a subsistence base to chicle production."[26]

General May, although a Mayan separatist, was acting like a traditional Mexican *cacique*.[26] Access to power, indeed to the authorities outside the region, was almost entirely in his hands. When the Mexican government was eventually able to remove him from the scene, it was partially because his authoritarian rule was no longer tolerable to his supporters, who wanted greater access to the benefits of a secular society—schools, hospitals, and freedom of movement. General May's removal from the scene represented an advance for the chicleros in the south of Quintana Roo, while those in the north, which May had not controlled, had already begun to assert their rights and independence. The wealth that was being created around chicle was concentrated in the hands of a couple of dozen contractors and intermediaries, who sold to the chewing gum companies and to entrepreneurs in Cozumel.[28]

In 1927 the Wrigley's company had made profits in the United States of $30 million, after tax. Almost half of the exports of chicle from Mexico came from Quintana Roo, and much of the rest was from the state of Yucatán. Not without reason, the Mexican consul at the border in British Honduras, Celso Perez Sandi, wrote in 1930, "The extraction of chicle was the only source of life for commerce in the region." He was referring to the physical and social infrastructure that the trade in gum was beginning to open up: towns, port facilities, schools, shops, and, with them, the arrival of new social groups without roots in the forest economy of the region.[29] The social revolution in Yucatán and particularly the frontier region of Quintana Roo, which had been controlled by *caciques* like General May, gradually gave way to a society grounded in the politics and morality of the postrevolutionary Mexican state.

As the Mexican state became more involved in the territory from which chicle was harvested, the unrest that had fueled the

Cruzoob resistance became channeled into more modern forms of social organization. The most prominent of these were the chicle cooperatives, which were established through the peninsula in the 1930s and 1940s. The government began to establish cooperatives among chicleros with the idea of freeing them from intermediaries and enabling them to sell directly to agents and companies. Under President Cardenas in the late 1930s the idea grew that chicleros should be more than itinerant workers with camps in the forest; they should be integrated into the land that provides their livelihood. This was a radical idea for forest communities, and particularly for the Maya. However, many of the chicleros who had arrived in the region from outside had little to do with Mayan autarchy.

On August 20, 1935, one of the first chicle cooperatives, Pucte, was founded with twenty-nine members. The co-op sold six tons of chicle directly to the Wrigley's company, increasing the income received by the chicleros threefold. The establishment of cooperatives brought collective strength to the organization of workers in the industry. In the same year cooperatives were established in Carrillo Puerto, Xhazil, Yaactun, Dzula, Xpichil, Senor, and Chumpon, all lucrative areas for the chicle trade. The governor of Yucatán at the time, Rafael Melgar, even made moves to expropriate large estates in the region, going so far as to bring one of them before a new agrarian commission. The apparent success of the cooperatives was making inroads on the established landlord class.

Once started, the move toward socialized production was very rapid.[30] Chicleros formed cooperatives because it enabled them to get both a better share and a better price for the resin through dealing directly with the buyers. Under the governorship of Melgar, an umbrella organization was established that took

The banks of the Rio Hondo, with a deserted chicle camp

control of the sale and export of the cooperatives' chicle, using both Chetumal and British Honduras as the ports of embarkation. Forty-eight chicle cooperatives had been formed, and this second-level organization had offices in Felipe Carrillo Puerto and Cozumel.

A much-quoted anecdote from this period illustrates the radical character of the new socialized units of production. President Cardenas is alleged to have asked an aide how much land chicleros needed to form a viable cooperative, and he was told that about 420 hectares would be sufficient. Partly as a consequence, many of the cooperatives that were formed subsequently in the zone were given legal jurisdiction over this amount of land.[31] Thus, although the Mayan rebellion had played such a central role in the fortunes of the chicle industry—especially near the border with British Honduras—by the 1930s the majority of chicleros who were not ethnically Mayan were now beholden to the Mexican state rather than to Mayan generals like Francisco May.

At the beginning of the 1940s, chicle production was given an additional boost by the entry of the United States into World War II. Within the space of a couple of years, chicle resin had assumed strategic importance. It was part of the GIs rations, and demand for it from the United States remained insatiable. The Mexican government authorized new concessions in the Yucatán Peninsula, which led to widespread exploitation of the forest, creaming off of many of the hardwoods, and the use of highly exploitative systems to remove the latex, which served to damage the remaining chicozapote trees.

In 1942 Mexico exported more chicle to the United States than at any time in its history: nearly 4 million kilos. This momentum in chicle production reached its apogee in June 1943, when a party of representatives of chicle cooperatives traveled to the United States to meet government officials. Their objective was "to discuss and defend the price of Mexican chicle, one of the most highly prized wartime materials in the United States." The American manufacturers, who in the view of the Mexican cooperatives merely "added the flavor" to the gum, had refused to increase the price they paid for it, and the producers wanted to be paid for their gum in gold rather than in U.S. dollars, given the apparent precariousness of the wartime financial markets.[32] The economic relations governing chicle took negotiations to the highest levels of the wartime American and Mexican administrations, such was the strategic importance of the product for both parties. The level of concentration in the gum industry had served to increase the companies' leverage over the U.S. government; most of the chicle exported from Mexico was bought by just three American companies.[33]

Despite the increased intervention of the Mexican federal authorities into most aspects of chicle production and marketing and the setting up of cooperatives among chicleros, the boom in production during wartime did not change most aspects of the way chicle was collected. As a rule, the chicleros continued to journey to the forest on foot, and chicle continued to be transported largely on the back of mules.

The Mayans' citadel of Noh Cah Balam Na Santa Cruz, where they had shed so much blood in defending it against the Mexican army of General Bravo in 1901, is today called Felipe Carrillo Puerto, after the former governor of Yucatán who was sympathetic to the Mayan cause in the 1920s and became a victim of assassination. It is, to all appearances, a modern town making a quiet living from agriculture and commerce, well outside the

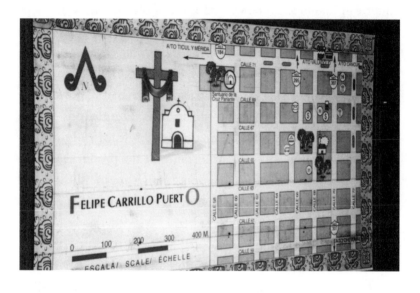

Map of Felipe Carrillo Puerto (formerly Chan Santa Cruz) showing the Cruzoob Talking Cross shrine

loop of mass tourism that dominates most of the Mexican Caribbean coast today. However, the town hides a secret that is closely connected with the fortunes of chewing gum. Within the urban contours of Felipe Carrillo Puerto today is a plot of land containing a church protected by a few devout Mayan families and dedicated to the memory of all the Mayan martyrs who died fighting the Mexican government for almost four centuries culminating in the Caste War.[34] For the Maya who live in the villages around Felipe Carrillo Puerto, the battle has never ended, even if most of their great-grandparents returned to their villages from the forests almost a century ago.

Today few tourists visit this shrine, and it can be difficult to find, but local people all know of its existence. Felipe Carrillo Puerto is one of five area villages that protect and house the Talking Cross, a powerful cultural emblem that nobody, even the most devout, is allowed to see and that represents the last vestiges of Mayan resistance to white rule. The Talking Cross is whispered about rather than discussed.[35] For while it is a part of everyday life for the devout rebel Maya, the Cruzoob, it remains a symbol of their resistance to white rule.

The next chapter examines the conditions under which chicle was collected in the forest and the experiences of the men and women who lived and worked there. For these people, chewing gum was a way of life.

4

A WAY OF LIFE

Most Mexicans first heard the news about chicle and the conditions under which it was produced in the forests of Yucatán through a series of newspaper articles by a young lawyer, Ramón Beteta. In 1929, when he was in his twenties, Beteta was sent to the sparsely populated eastern frontier of the Yucatán Peninsula as a member of an official government mission. Before his account of the production and sale of the resin, the source of chewing gum had been shrouded in mystery. As we have seen, Quintana Roo, at the time of Beteta's arrival, had only recently become part of the new revolutionary Mexico, and not until 1929 was the regional *cacique* and Mayan leader General May forced by the federal government to make political concessions to Mexico City.

Even after 1929 most of the territory of Quintana Roo was barely accessible from the outside. Beteta and his friends arrived by boat in Payo Obispo (today's Chetumal), and their journey into the interior was undertaken either by foot or on mules. Like many frontier areas of Latin America today, Quintana Roo in the 1920s was a wild amalgam of recent immigrants, indigenous peoples, and reluctant officials who felt they had been cast out of "civilized society." Beteta almost despaired of bringing any sanity to what he saw as a deprived and recalcitrant population. But he could see that absence of civilization was linked to the social and economic vulnerability of the chicleros themselves. It was economic necessity that had forced people to abandon their homes and leave other parts of tropical Mexico, like the area of Tuxpan in the state of Veracruz, for the uncertainties of remote forests held by a rebel Mayan army. Among the Mayan chicleros it was also the need to supplement the meager cash income they might receive from agriculture. As we have seen, the Mayan forces grew more dependent on the cash income they received from selling chicle to intermediaries. It corrupted some of the chiefs, and ordinary workers became much more dependent on the money economy.

The chicleros' way of life was intimately connected with the forest, as well as with the market intermediaries to whom they sold. Their contact with the chewing gum companies, most of them American, was very limited. They were hired or contracted for the season by an intermediary who sold their resin to the companies. Although part of the transformation of resin into gum was undertaken by the chicleros, their control of the commercialization process was negligible. The forest concessions won by the contractors allowed them freedoms denied to the chicle tappers who, until the rise of cooperatives and stable prices, were continually indebted.

The steps that were taken to open up the forests not only changed the lives of the people who depended immediately on their products, but also changed the face of Quintana Roo. Within the space of fifty years or so, most of the high forests where the chicozapote tree grew had been removed or transformed into lower, secondary forest where the vegetation had regrown. This was particularly the case closer to Merida and the rest of Mexico. The destruction of the primary forest could not be laid at the door of the chicleros—they merely cut a path through. What succeeded them was a radical shift in land-use patterns, as agriculture and cattle production took over and more roads were built. The chicleros were merely early links in a chain that eventually brought both national and international capital to bear on the forest economy and, with it, serious implications for tropical ecology. As we see in chapter 7, the role of extractive forest industries, including the harvesting of chicle, still has enormous relevance for development in the region today.

The Harvesting of Chicle

The tree from which chicle was derived, the chicozapote tree, grows in the forests of the Yucatán Peninsula in Mexico and the neighboring countries of Belize and Guatemala. It is found deep in the jungle, where it grows to a height of ten to fifteen meters and is interspersed with other hardwoods such as mahogany. The diameter of the trunk of the mature tree is about one to one and a half meters thick, and it takes about eight to ten years to mature sufficiently to be tapped. Most of the foliage forms a canopy, which envelops the forest. The wood of the chicozapote is reddish in color, hard, and can be used to make furniture. The fruit (the *sapodilla*), sweet and deliciously pungent, from which the native Maya made a form of custard.

Although the chicozapote produces numerous seeds hidden in the bulbous and fleshy fruit and can reproduce itself very rapidly,

A chiclero using machete to cut tree

tree growth is relatively slow, making it a vulnerable member of the forest species community. If the bark is tough it can be tapped after a rest period of four to five years, but trees with more delicate bark need much longer to recover, typically ten years or more. The quantity of resin that can be derived from a single tree also varies widely, from about three kilos to as much as fifteen kilos. Normally the tree is tapped for twelve to twenty-four hours at one time.[1] Tapping it for longer periods carries the risk of destroying it. The resin itself is a white, milky color, with the consistency of elastic. To the taste it is insipid, and the quality of the sap depends critically on the amount of water it contains: The more diluted the resin, the less valuable it is commercially, since its manufacture requires it to be boiled to remove moisture.

The tree can only be tapped during the wet season, running from July until January, when high daily temperatures complement heavy rain and force the tree to sweat. This was the work season for the chicleros, when they left their villages behind and set off for the deepest recesses of the forest. Initially they located in base camps of perhaps twenty or thirty men, sleeping in hammocks in simple huts, with a small number of women—often family members—to do their cooking. This constituted the epicenter of their social life for much of the year. During the day the chicleros, in groups of five or six men, fanned out farther into the woods and made small clearings (or *hatos*) in the forest.

In the early morning, long before the sun reached its full intensity, the chicleros left their huts on foot and began the task of locating the four or five trees that they intended to tap that day. To establish whether the trees were capable of producing enough latex, they made several small incisions into the bark. Having identified the tree he wished to tap, the chiclero made a V-shaped

Tapping chicle

cut in the bark at the bottom of the trunk, gradually taking the incision higher and higher, until he was climbing the tree, suspended by ropes. Eventually the cuts ascended to the tree canopy, forming a zigzag design from the crown of the tree to the ground below. A canvas pouch or bag was placed at the bottom of the tree, and the latex was collected in this during the next twenty hours or so, after which it was transported in sacks back to the clearing or camp. Here it was reduced, boiled down in large copper vats to remove the excess water, the trick being to reduce the liquid without actually burning the resin. The resin was then transferred to brown-colored, brick-shaped *marquetas,* or molds, each of which contained between eight and ten kilos of solid latex. These molds enabled the latex to be handled easily and transported back to the contractor, usually on the backs of mules.

The conditions under which most chicleros lived during the first three decades of the century were lamentable; they were routinely exposed to considerable risk and danger apart from their financial vulnerability. In the forest they were prey to diseases and infections, to attack from snakes and other animals, and to the bites of the chiclero fly, an insect that lived in the tree canopy and attacked the inner ear, producing facial deformations and the ulcers for which the chicleros were known (*leishmaniasis* or chiclero ear). Accidents high in the forest canopy were also common, with so much work being undertaken on improvised ropes. Accidents were made worse by alcoholism. As we have seen already, alcoholism was almost endemic by the 1920s, evidenced by the territory of Quintana Roo formally adopting prohibition laws.

The financial precariousness and vulnerability of the chicleros made their lives even worse. They lived for six or seven months of the year on a cash advance which was paid them by a contractor

A chiclero using a machete to cut a tree

Preparing to cook chicle resin

Chiclero with *marqueta* or brick of solid gum

who undertook to buy their chicle at an agreed price. The quantity of chicle that each chiclero handed over to the contractor was entered into the accounting system at the end of each season, and the cost of the provisions and material that had been advanced to him was subtracted. This system, which has its parallels throughout Latin America in the form of *enganche* or "tied" labor, was open to constant abuse and led to inevitable indebtedness on the part of chicleros. They were not wage laborers, like many rural workers, but they were not peasants in the classic sense either because they owned neither their means of production nor their land. Their position was most similar to that of sharecroppers, who effectively worked in competition with one another for a share of the market under onerous conditions dictated by the person, or company, to whom they sold their crop.[2]

As we have seen, the majority of the first chicleros were not Mayan, although Mayan workers joined the industry from the 1920s onward. They came mostly from other tropical regions, such as Tamaulipas, Campeche, and Chiapas, although most came from the area around Tuxpan, Veracruz. Their arrival in Quintana Roo in vast numbers served to underline the process through which a distinctive Mayan culture, which had chosen to turn its back on the dubious benefits of civilization, became culturally integrated into postrevolutionary Mexico. The chiclero invasion proved more effective than the Mexican state in nationalizing the forest frontier of the Yucatán Peninsula and ensuring that the Mexican national identity was dominant.

For many chicleros, especially in the first two decades of the new century, conditions were so appalling that they sought sanctuary elsewhere. The position of chicleros who abandoned work in the forest and sought exile across the border in British Honduras at

A chiclero in the forest

the beginning of this period was summarized in an article in the newspaper *The Clarion,* published in 1905:

> A large number of chicleros, members of different company gangs, from the other side of the Rio Hondo, have deserted their place of work, for one reason or another, and have reached Corozal and other parts of our colony. These men are not only useless as laborers, but are also highly dangerous and undesirable as immigrants. They can easily be distinguished by the enormous straw hats they wear, like bell-towers, and by their contemptible and dirty appearance. It appears that in Corozal they make a living by begging from house to house, and selling whatever trifle they can get their hands on. They have filled the prisons and hospitals to overflowing with asylum-seekers. They can easily be treated as destitute immigrants, who have arrived by sea, compelled to seek refuge, but there is no alternative but to rid ourselves of those who arrive on foot, in groups of two or three, or singly. There are some, nevertheless, who want to work here, but only a small minority who, by being so exceptional serve to demonstrate the undeserving nature of the great majority.[3]

Subsequently, reports circulated about chicleros who had been expelled from their forest clearings by contractors when they fell ill. Those who were fit enough to travel found their way to British Honduras, while the corpses of others were discovered on the road to Bacalar, in the south of the territory. These problems eventually led the Mexican government to insist that the companies that employed chicleros issue them with written contracts and that their state governments undertake to return them to their homeland to prevent further disastrous attempts at exile. The worst abuses continued, however, and it was not until much later that the conditions for chicleros began to improve gradually. When this did happen it was not so much because of humanitarian concern as a breakthrough in technology. New machinery for logging hardwoods enabled this operation to be undertaken at any time of the year, creating a synergy with chicle collection. This changed the orientation of the chicleros' work in some ways—they began to play a larger part in forest clearance, as well as logging and chicle collection. Rather than return from the high forest to their homes on a seasonal basis, they began bringing their families with them into the newly cleared zones.

Tierra del Chicle

One of the few contemporary accounts of the lives of chicleros was provided by the young lawyer Ramón Beteta in a series of articles for the press at the beginning of the 1930s, just as chicle was entering a boom period. These articles later became a book, *Tierra del Chicle,* which was first published in 1951 (and reprinted in a new edition in 1999, to celebrate the twenty-fifth anniversary of the founding of the state of Quintana Roo). The book is an important contribution to the recent history of frontiers and provides useful insights into the way chicle was viewed during the boom years and its subsequent role in the transformation of the forest. It is infused with a modernizing energy, generated by the aspirations of the Mexican Revolution, to bring the benefits of civilization to the most remote corners of the republic. In Quintana Roo few of the men who had spent their working lives deep in the inhospitable forest left land titles to their dependents. *Tierra del Chicle* provides a snapshot of a way of life that was to disappear within the space of a few decades, as the social anarchy of Mexico's tropics was replaced by political mobilization and state social engineering.

Mexico was just emerging from the darkest days of its revolution when Beteta and his colleagues left for Quintana Roo. Not until the late 1920s did Mexican social and political life begin to normalize following a series of internecine battles and threats from abroad. Much of the pain was self-inflicted, and, like most civil wars, the Mexican Revolution left long-standing, and bitter divisions within the population. Beteta's documentation of the life of chicleros was motivated by what he saw as a need for more social inclusivity, for setting out clearly the social degradation to which an itinerant and dependent population had been driven. In his view, the new federal government should champion the cause of the chicleros by absorbing this abandoned region fully into the new civil society that was being created. In *Tierra del Chicle,* and his earlier book *Jarana,* Beteta saw himself as an active protagonist in the modernization of his country.[4]

Beteta identifies three groups during his extended visit to Quintana Roo in 1929: Mayan Indians, chicleros, and public employees. His sympathies lay with the last two. The native inhabitants of the forest had similar characteristics, in his view, to those of the forest itself. He begins by trying to think of the forest as "a huge Chapultepec (Park) . . . the new part of the Park, made up of artificial woods . . . without the cement, and much muddier." Chapultepec is the Central Park of Mexico City, the lungs of the city, but any similarity with the jungles of Quintana Roo seems remote. This is one of many allusions in which Beteta demonstrates that the forest needs to be brought within the fold of civilization. He demonstrates that he has designs on the wilderness he found outside him. The group arrived in the forest without any clear expectations, just romantic images. As another member of Beteta's party claimed, "We had imagined a fantastic

The original title page of *Tierra del Chicle*

Chicleros in the forest, from Beteta (*Tierra del Chicle*)

Chicleros, from Beteta

tropical jungle, but we found a torpid and monotonous forest, lacking in hope."[5]

Beteta constantly uses one metaphor in his account of the dense jungles of Quintana Roo: The forest, like the people who inhabited it, had built defenses against invasion. He believed you can better understand the mystery of the forest if you look upon it as a system designed to keep out strangers, or "unknown ene-mies." "The trees are a line of defense; those which have spines give off corrosive liquids, or their fruit is poisonous, or they cut you on contact, or their shade sends you to sleep."[6] It was a forbidding and largely unintelligible environment to the twenty-four-year-old Beteta, newly arrived from Mexico City.

Most of Beteta's imagery suggests the hostility of the forest, and there is little in his account to suggest it is anybody's home. He tells the story of a chiclero who is bitten by a venomous snake and, following tradition, bites the snake in return, hoping to neutralize its venom. Unfortunately the man does not survive, and on one of the myriad footpaths through the forest, his body is found with the snake curled around him, in a mutual, and deadly, embrace. Elsewhere he speaks of giant ants eating a huge locust that "resembled one of the toy airplanes they sell in the Main Square in Mexico City."[7] He sees vast white vultures flying overhead, wings wide enough to cast shadows on the forest clear-ings, and orange-colored tarantulas underfoot, making every step through the forest a hazard.

Everywhere there is putrefaction in the forest. He is terrorized by the sight of a putrefied crocodile being eaten by vultures, and he cannot rid himself of the memory of this image. He thinks this might be because the smell of fermenting matter attacks the senses and confuses the mind. Every step of the forest represents a step toward oblivion and madness. He recounts the story of another chiclero from the banks of the Rio Hondo who leaves the footpath in pursuit of a wild turkey, soon finding that he has lost his way. Eight days later, the same man wanders into a forest clearing, where there is a hut; he walks "as if in a dream, with the body of the decomposed turkey around his neck."[8] The forest is not enslaved by man, but the forest enslaves man. In the end, the forest "always wins." He gives as example forest clearings, which, even after one season of neglect, are subject to rapid forest regrowth.

There is little sympathy for the Mayan Indian in Beteta's account. He comments that the Indians want to go unnoticed, to blend into the jungle, rather than do anything to make it more habitable. In comparison, the chiclero is a romantic, if impoverished, figure. The Indian is ignorant and indifferent to the jungle; he is as inaccessible and uncomprehending as the jungle itself. The *mestizo* (mixed race) chiclero, on the other hand, is depicted in modernist hue; his way of life resists the jungle and seeks to civilize it. The chiclero provides a Promethean opening for development by refusing to bend to nature. Unlike the Indian, the chicleros could live elsewhere; they simply lack the means to do so. The native Maya, however, "is nomadic and antisocial, unable to domesticate animals and live from stockholding, nor even able to domesticate plants in a way that permits a decent standard of living."[9] Such passages demonstrate ignorance and prejudice in equal proportions and confirm the suspicion that Beteta is using preconceived and racist views to buttress his idea of progress. He seems to be saying that the magnitude and hostility of the forest environment undermines social progress in the chiclero and denies it entirely to those who "belong" there, the Indians.

When, eventually, he meets the chicleros in their encampments, Beteta records them as being "proud" of their attempts to improve their lot by forming cooperatives. Their camp has a "military air," disciplined and focused on work, and most of the activities are shared responsibilities. The chiclero, in Beteta's view, combines a measure of individualism and independence with some of the benefits of living collectively. The absence of a direct employer, to whom he must pay daily attention, and the freedom to roam in the forest have, according to Beteta, given the chiclero the character of a free spirit. This is quite unlike most of the agricultural peons in the Mexico of his day. Chicleros in the forest remind him of sailors out of port, living through terrible privations until their "orgy of spending"—when the season is over and they return to the towns and spend a year's earnings in a few days.

The object of the chicleros' labors, chicle itself, is not altogether an attractive one, in Beteta's judgment. He notes that the resin is "sweet, sticky, with an astringent effect on lips and tongue, and an acrid smell." As the chiclero harvests the resin, he sweats profusely, taking on the appearance of the tree he is tapping. Both man and tree seem to sweat and suffer together; both seem "possessed by the same unconsciousness, and moved by the same fate."

Eventually Beteta and his companions arrive at the former capital of the rebel Maya, Santa Cruz de Bravo (Felipe Carrillo Puerto). It is 1929, and he finds the town in a neglected state, abandoned by civilization. The town of Santa Cruz had only 240 inhabitants. It was isolated from the "civilized world" and lacked "culture." Most of the people who were not born in the region but lived there longed to escape. The only hope for the town, and the region, was better communications. Santa Cruz is "ultimately a place of exile for Mexicans and Mayans, who are not yet reconciled to the heat of the Revolution."[10] It is the capital of a "country full of adventurers," ruled over, with diminished efficacy, by the inscrutable General May.

Beteta begs to differ from those who view May as a corrosive force. By 1929 he was principally viewed as a chicle contractor, rather than as the leader of a revolutionary army. General May now traveled hundreds of miles in his work, supported by the patronage of the Mexican state. He was no longer a religious chief, and the tribes he is supposed to have led are largely a "fantasy," in Beteta's words.

This account of the "land of chicle" is intriguing and important for a number of reasons. It represents a white Mexican's view of a region that had been fought over for centuries. It had entered the modern world through an artifact—chewing gum—which had to be stripped from trees under desperate human conditions. The land in which the gum was harvested was inhospitable to whites but was home to thousands of Maya; they were two mutually incomprehensible cultures. The only solution to the backwardness of the region, in the view of modernizers like Beteta, was to integrate it into Mexico proper. The only solution for the chiclero was "to make of the individual adventurer a responsible collective being." With this paradox, Beteta finishes his book.

The consequences of resolving this paradox led in different directions in different successive periods. First, the challenge of reducing individual vulnerabilities and social exclusion led to the collectivized politics of the 1930s, 1940s, and 1950s, when the political party identified with the Mexican state (the Party of the Institutional Revolution [PRI]) acted as patron to the workers whose loyalty it commanded, in return for largesse. Later, during the 1980s and 1990s, during the periods of deregulation and market liberalization, the "individual adventurer" was cast in the role of entrepreneur. Chicle cooperatives employed commercial operatives to help them identify markets for their product, even at a time when demand for chicle and other forest products was in decline.

The Cooperative Movement

We have seen how some of the rebel Maya, despite the oppression to which they had ultimately submitted, were able to profit from the forests by occupying a key position in regional struggles for resources and power. Through the sale of chicle, they were able until the 1930s to keep the Mexican state at a distance and to renew their own efforts at autonomy and separation. At the same time, the half-century between 1900 and 1950 marked a period in which Mayans all but disappeared from the political landscape of the territory now known as Quintana Roo. The importance of chicle as an economic activity cast the forests in a different light. The forests of the east and south of the Yucatán Peninsula were viewed as empty forests, devoid of inhabitants. This was particularly true of the most remote regions where, before the arrival of chicleros in the 1940s and 1950s, power lay in the hands of traders and *haciendas*.[11] The challenge for the Mexican state was to bring civilization to these areas, in the form of roads, rural schools, and political organization.

Clues to this disappearance of the Maya from the historical account lie in the changing fortunes of the chicle industry and the way in which it began to take up a more central space in the rhetoric of Mexican national development. Chicle provoked internal divisions among Mayan leaders but it also led, as Beteta's prose demonstrates, to modernizing solutions. Mexico could only progress by colonizing the forests and converting them, in one form or another, to productive use. Chicle and timber extraction began the process that would be completed by the federal government's vast tourist investments in Cancún and the surrounding coast from the 1970s onward.

The genesis of these processes was established by President Cardenas, who made chiclero cooperatives part of the national land reform that he energetically pursued in the 1930s. The chicleros had built a raw society from the forest communities they established, and with it a social structure that very few outsiders could comprehend. Many of the chicleros interviewed in Calakmul by Ponce Jimenez, a Mexican anthropologist, describe a society that was as exciting as it was dangerous. These people measured esteem in terms of accomplishments that few outside the closed circle could fully appreciate, such as knowledge of forest ecology and skill in climbing trees or using machetes. In the course of their work, chicleros became accomplished hunters and honed survival skills that enabled them to withstand appalling deprivation and danger. Many became very aware of the vulnerability of their environment. In the forest they experienced almost permanent food scarcity, and in the town they experienced constant indebtedness. But they also experienced periods of the year when they held surplus disposable income, and other periods when they possessed the independence to dispose of it. Fifty years later, in the 1990s, chicleros described a nightmare world not unlike the world of magical realism in Latin American fiction:

> Calakmul chiclero families still keep in mind men who made
> pacts with forest spirits to increase their harvest, monkeys who

fell in love with camp cooks, anteaters who dared men to test their
strength in arm-wrestling contests, and jaguars who, placing their
paws in a man's own footsteps, silently followed chicleros through
the forest.[12]

Observations like these, which draw heavily on Mayan ideas
about the forest and the intimate relations that exist between
animals and humans, are virtually absent from official accounts
of the forest economy of the period.

The historical account of chicleros contains few observations
on the supernatural life of the forest, or the power of myth, since
few historians had recourse to the experiences and imagination of
the chicleros. It is dominated by the fortunes of the cooperatives'
workers and the political machinations of generations of regional
leaders, or *caciques.* In many of these accounts, the more important
officials in the cooperative movement matched the duplicity and
corruption of foreigners and intermediaries in the wider chewing
gum market.[13]

The chicle industry shifted from a remote forest economy of
resource extraction, mediated by Mexican and American entrepreneurs, to a dependency of the Mexican state through several
formative steps. The cooperative movement came to fruition for
most chicleros under President Cardenas, who visited Quintana
Roo for the first time at the end of November 1939. He had
already called on chiclero support during his campaign for office
four years earlier. In August 1936 he gave his blessing to the first
official chiclero cooperative, established in 1935 in the village of
Pucte on the banks of Rio Hondo. Cardenas also established a
state fund to help nascent cooperatives in the region. From the
standpoint of its members, this cooperative was an experiment in
practical socialism. Chicle resin would be owned collectively and

Chicle cooperative today

marketed through the government of the territory. Their intention was to break free from the intermediaries and contractors who had control over chicle and its commercialization. The first manager of the cooperative Pucte was a highly regarded rural schoolmaster and pioneer of cooperatives, Rodolfo Baeza.

The chicleros from Pucte worked hard to organize and provision themselves, carrying supplies by mule into the forest clearings (*hatos*) and transporting the resin back to the banks of the Rio Hondo. Their sacrifices, however, were not in vain, and through bypassing the intermediaries, each cooperative member received more than twice as much for each kilogram of resin as that of wage laborers, which itself helped to stimulate interest among other chicleros in the benefits of joining the cooperative movement.

As one might expect, the successes of the cooperative at Pucte did not go unnoticed by the private entrepreneurs in chicle, who recognized that their interest in monopolizing chicle production might be threatened. This, in turn, prompted a sympathetic President Cardenas to place the organization of cooperatives under the direct control of the government of the territory, which would be in a stronger position to counter the pressures mounted by the private sector. By 1940, there were forty-three chicle cooperatives with more than two thousand members in the region. To the chicleros, at this moment, the cooperative movement became even more closely associated with the fortunes—and failings—of the Mexican state. At an inaugural meeting held in Chetumal in March 1940, the Federation of Cooperatives of Workers and Peasants in Quintana Roo came into being, with the express objective of bringing together coop-eratives made up of both Mayan and non-Mayan members throughout the territory. Thenceforth, the cooperative movement

Building in Peto, headquarters of chicle trading in the north

among chicleros and workers in the lumber industry was so closely connected with government and resource exploitation in the region that it was often impossible to distinguish it from the state. The industry, which had blossomed under family entrepreneurship and enterprise in the United States, had acquired a completely different character in Mexico. In Mexico, like many other countries in Latin America at the time, socialist organizations had grown up to defend workers from the ravages of the market. The chicleros of Yucatán were now foot soldiers in a socialist movement and strong supporters of a populist and left-leaning president.

But first the chicleros were delivered into the hands of the new organs of state management and control, represented by Mexico's PRI. When President Avila Camacho took over for Cardenas in 1940, a new governor, Gabriel Guevara, was appointed for the territory of Quintana Roo and was much less sympathetic to the chicleros' movement than his predecessor, Rafael Melgar, had been. With the connivance of Guevara, a vote of censure was passed on the cooperative movement, and systematic efforts were made to weaken the popular support of its leaders. Until 1958, the governor of Yucatán, Margarito Ramirez, a supporter of Guevara, made it his business to encourage the wholesale exploitation of the territory's forests, lining the pockets of his supporters and dispossessing the cooperatives of their funds. This reflected tendencies throughout Mexican politics as the PRI established its power base, tendencies that had never been completely erased under the reforming administration of Cardenas. The chiclero cooperative movement also suffered a double blow in these years. In the 1950s, it was not only subjected to human exploitation, it also suffered from the depredations of nature. Hurricane Janet devastated much of the south

Chicleros in a forest camp, early 1900s

coast of the Caribbean, laying waste to important sources of chicle and leaving embattled, fragile communities in ruins.

A decade later, in 1969, the fortunes of the Federation of Cooperatives began to improve again under the organization's first leader from Quintana Roo, Jose Asencio. During the long period of attrition, the cooperatives had lost much of their social insurance function, and unscrupulous politicians had pillaged their medical and life insurance funds. Under Jose Asencio this process was reversed, and the cooperatives began to cover medical expenses and provide life insurance once more. To some extent this reflected a modest reversal in the fortunes of the industry, with chicle exports doubling between 1964 and 1973, and more chicle being exported to countries other than the United States, to Japan and Italy in particular. This enabled the chicleros to benefit from a more effectively regulated industry. In 1971 the Banco Nacional de Comercio Exterior, together with the chicle cooperatives, was able to negotiate a better price for its resin from its principal market in the United States, Wrigley's. One of the principal organs of the Mexican state was acting for a group of workers during a period when their industry was in decline and the demand for natural chicle-based gum was lower than it had ever been. Ironically, during the period of boom in the industry, when the American companies like Wrigley's depended heavily on Mexican imports, the chicleros had nobody protecting their wages or conditions of work.

Local Entrepreneurs and Survivors

Don Ignacio Merocer is in his late sixties and lives in Valladolid, in a large modern house to the north of the city. Today he still makes a living selling water from a purification plant attached to his house. His hobby is to take his pickup van, loaded with ropes and plastic containers, into a stretch of forest that he still owns, some fifty miles from his home. He usually leaves early in the morning and arrives back late the same night, spending the day tapping chicle from chicozapote trees and distilling the contents with his equipment into one of the large plastic containers he carries. He is experimenting with chicle, convinced that it has a future in a world increasingly dedicated to preserving the natural and the organic, and he is interested in the preservation of the lifestyles usually associated with these terms. Don Ignacio's ambition, he says, is to advertise his chicle on the World Wide Web and to take small groups of interested people for day trips deep into the remaining forest, inland from the coastal village of Akumal. He wants to pave a new path within ecotourism.

Whether or not chicle has a future for Don Ignacio, it certainly had a past. His father had been a gum contractor during the 1950s and 1960s, working a concession three days outside of Valladolid on mule back, near a village called Chuletan. The principal camp for his activities was close to the Caribbean, near Akumal, which is today a favored location for divers, bathers, and fishermen. In the days when, as a young man, he helped his father in his business, they spent three or four months each year at this camp and the eight subsidiary camps, managing a workforce of more than two hundred chicleros. There was a small staff at the principal camp throughout the season to look after the needs of the workers and their foreman (or *capitaz*), whose main job was to verify the quality of the chicle produced. By the 1950s, these camps had grown in sophistication compared with those described by Beteta thirty years earlier, and by the time of Don

Ignacio, the men were buying their own provisions rather than having their living costs deducted from their advances. He claims proudly that one of his first innovations when he took over from his father in the early 1960s was to increase the men's wages, from which they had to buy their own provisions. Until then, the chicleros had their food and necessities provided for them during the winter period in the forest, and they were paid only after the resin had been collected and sold, making them indebted to the contractor.

His father had started out as a *contratista* in 1958 when, after several unsuccessful attempts, he managed to secure a concession to exploit the forest from an agricultural engineer he knew who was well connected with the government. By this time the Federation of Chicle Cooperatives was a major force not only in the production of chicle but also in its marketing and export. He and his father were given permission to tap 20,000 kilos of chicle in the first year of their concession, a quota that they easily exceeded, producing 28,000 kilos. Don Ignacio soon showed a flair for the business and, after working unpaid for five years, took over the family business from his father at the young age of twenty-seven. The annual figures for chicle produced from his concession varied widely, partly depending on how wet the winter season had been, but in 1978 he became the champion for the territory of Quintana Roo, producing 140,000 kilos, 20,000 more than the quota. By this time he was contracting more than seven hundred men, operating out of twenty-eight forest camps.

Talking to Don Ignacio today, one is left with the impression that the chicle cooperatives were in a weak position to develop their enterprises in the directions prompted by the export market. In his view chicle was always better organized as a private enterprise than on a wholly cooperative basis. This was because locally organized cooperatives and *ejidos*, with access to community or nationally owned land, inevitably put the social necessities of their members before their competitive efficiency. While he was in the industry, the Federation of Chicle Cooperatives had been responsible for checking the quality of the resin and controlled the allocation of concessions on behalf of the Mexican government, but the industry had always been a combination of cooperatives and private businesses. The cooperatives never had enough surplus profits to invest in better methods of collection, processing, and storage, which were all being transformed during the period Don Ignacio was in the industry. The very social objective of the co-ops, to improve workers' standards of living, made them unsuitable organizations for meeting new economic challenges and for accumulating funds with which the organization could diversify out of dependence on chicle and into newer, more lucrative markets.

Don Ignacio spends summer evenings dancing the *jarana* and other local dances of Yucatán in the town square, where he is regarded as a man of substance as well as something of a local expert on chicle. There are other retired contractors living in Valladolid whose experiences are derived from earlier periods in the industry—the 1940s and 1950s—when the conditions prevailing bore more resemblance to those described by Ramón Beteta. These are men whom chewing gum treated well. They live in substantial houses built in part with the labor of many tens of thousands of workers, whose exploitative conditions of life helped provide for their fortunes. The successful entrepreneurs are celebrated today as examples of family ingenuity and dedication. At the same time, chicleros populate the villages of the zone. They are very old now but, like their former employers, are part of the collective memory, and selective amnesia, that has accompanied the chewing gum industry in Yucatán and Quintana Roo.

Conclusion

The way of life represented by chicleros, contractors, and all those involved in the gum industry disappeared slowly from the forests of Yucatán. The shifts in resources and land use that were prompted by the opening up of the tropical frontier and the drive to extract chicle handed power to new groups of entrepreneurs who had nothing to do with chewing gum. The period of substantial chicle extraction stretched from the 1880s until the late 1950s, but the significance of chicle for Mexico lay partly in the way it opened up the previously inaccessible tropical forests. Chicle extractors cut paths into the forest, but they did not clear it. Those who followed them contributed materially to the forest destruction: Mahogany and cedar stands were depleted throughout the region, except in the most inaccessible or protected areas like the Calakmul Biosphere Reserve, on the border with Guatemala.

Of even more importance was the arrival of settlers, a product of Mexican government programs to encourage colonization in the 1970s and 1980s. These people used the existing road infrastructure, primitive as it was, to clear the forests of trees and cultivate *milpa*. Other government programs encouraged them to grow rice, although the groundwater resources of the limestone peninsula were always fragile and their limited usefulness for agriculture was often not fully understood. The rice programs proved, like so many other development solutions, to be short lived and expendable.[14]

Don Ignacio, chicle enthusiast, in 2002

Some government-sponsored programs, like those of cattle ranching and rice cultivation, were eventually abandoned, but they had already succeeded in opening up the territory further.

Whether stimulated by the government or by foreign capital, loggers and settlers gradually eroded the forests of the Yucatán Peninsula. The *selva mediana,* or upland forest, where most of the chicozapote trees grew, was also seriously degraded by the 1970s. In the case of some products, notably mahogany and cedar, there is evidence of this depletion from the closing of sawmills. As colonization progressed and forestry industries declined, the areas previously dedicated to extractive forest products, such as chicle, were rededicated to commercial agriculture and stock rearing. The dirt roads of the 1940s and 1950s made way for the paved roads of the 1970s and 1980s, and with improved infrastructure came still more immigrants.

The role of foreign capital, from the perspective of Mexico, had been essentially that "of a neo-colonial state, where resources were 'mined' from a former European colony in order to feed the industrial machine of the First World."[15] When the tables were turned to a limited extent and foreign private capital was replaced by the Mexican state, it made little difference in the degree of control exercised over natural resources by local communities. The working conditions of chicleros improved throughout the 1960s and 1970s, under the embrace of the state, but local control over valuable forest resources was kept to a minimum. Either substitutes had been found for forest products, which meant that they lost their market value (chicle), or the resources had become so rare that they were too expensive to obtain (mahogany). Frequently both processes were at work simultaneously. Mexican forestry policy had much more to do with national economic

Former chicle contractor in retirement

planning—which essentially meant resource extraction—than with nature conservation or the delegation of local management to local communities.[16]

Primary extractive industries, such as chicle production, often occupy marginal spaces in the global atlas, appearing almost randomly in the historical narratives of globalization. They have been described as spaces of "commodity supply," which provision distant consumers through a largely invisible network of complex economic and cultural relations. They are called "shadow-lands," created in the shadow of new consumer products and tastes but abandoned as easily as they were occupied.[17]

The social and cultural métier of the chiclero, once considered a way of life, not least by those practicing it, is usually excluded from more broad narratives about modernity and progress. In the aptly named epoch of postscarcity, the era of mass consumption in which we live today, the human agent is the one who consumes, not the one who produces. At times, of course, their singular fates coincide. In the case of chewing gum, a consumer culture developed as far removed from the forests of Yucatán as is possible to imagine. The people who consumed gum played a role on the stage of history that many could not have envisioned, such as service personnel in wartime living and working overseas. The gum they took with them had already made its mark in ways that could not have been anticipated. It had graduated from the publicity machines of Hollywood and global celebrity to the theaters of conflict.

5

B U B B L E   G U M   C U L T U R E S

The organization of chicle camps in the forests of Yucatán took little account of trends in consumption back in the United States. There chewing gum had become a fact of life and, as we have seen, a vehicle for promoting sports, celebrity, and national identity. The paraphernalia of mass society was being brought to bear on its marketing and promotion: neon lighting, baseball cards, vending machines, and celebrity endorsement. Before the United States entered World War II, the principal issue for gum manufacturers was how to market their product effectively, to the maximum number of people. Chewing gum had previously been viewed as a seasonal product: Sales picked up in the spring and remained high until the fall. During the Depression years of the 1930s, the chewing gum manufacturers looked for opportunities to use innovative marketing and promotion to brighten up the bleakness of peoples' everyday lives. In the subsequent decade, the 1940s, chewing gum was to occupy a new role, as an element in the service ration. In addition, the promotion of bubble gum opened up a new world full of exciting new marketing and sales possibilities for the manufacturers.

Bubble Gum Makes an Appearance

One of these companies, the American Chicle Company, which in the 1930s made a number of leading brands, including Blackjack, Dentyne, and Clove, began the long association with sex in marketing gum by hiring scores of attractive young women as sampling girls.[1] They were dressed in orange satin costumes and took to the streets of New York, offering free samples of gum to anybody they met. The company told the girls to give away five thousand pieces of chewing gum a day. Indeed, in the course of one year in the 1930s, they managed to part company with free samples to more than 1 and a half million New Yorkers. The impact of American Chicle's sales campaign was dramatic. Not for the last time in the history of chewing gum, sexual allure, combined with the appearance of sexual innocence, was highly effective in product merchandising.

The company founded by William Wrigley responded in kind. When Wrigley died in 1932 at the age of seventy, he was one of the ten wealthiest men in America. One of his sons, Philip, took over for his father and threw himself energetically into the campaign to capture the hearts and mouths of America. Philip Wrigley dressed his staff as opinion pollsters, itself a new phenomenon at the time, and sent them out across the country dressed as "Mr. Spear" and "Mr. Mint," offering a dollar to anyone who could answer a spot question correctly. To win the prize, of course, the person had to be in possession of an open packet of Wrigley's Spearmint gum. After sampling tens of thousands of members of the public and giving away thousands of dollars between 1932 and 1935, the promotion ended with the pollsters' report, which found that, among its many benefits, chewing gum was popular because it succeeded in relieving nervous tension.[2] Again a new technique, opinion polling, had been brought to bear on the marketing of gum, to enhance its appeal and to stake out new ground with innovative marketing.

The prewar period had been one of accelerated growth for the large gum manufacturers. In the 1920s Americans bought $100 million worth of chewing gum a year, a figure that increased markedly through the subsequent decade. By 1941, when the United States entered World War II, American kids were spending considerable sums of their own money on gum. Indeed, bubble gum, which had officially been invented by Walter Diemer in 1928, accounted for $4.5 million in sales by 1941.

The invention of bubble gum represented a watershed in the close association between chicle and chewing gum. In the early part of the twentieth century, when Adams and Wrigley were beginning to make great commercial strides in the chewing gum market, another businessman with foresight, Frank H. Fleer, developed the first prototype of bubble gum. Fleer had worked for his father-in-law, a candy manufacturer, but took over the business in 1880 and managed to change the factory into a chewing gum company, manufacturing gum for the first time in 1885. Already the market was crowded with rival manufacturers and products, and Fleer decided that to distinguish his gum from that of others, he should concentrate on one that could be blown into large bubbles.

Bubble gum differs from regular chewing gum in a number of ways that were to prove decisive in the future history of chicle-based gum. The usual gum bases that manufacturers had provided for decades were not suitable for producing bubbles. Spruce gum was too tiring on the jaw and paraffin gum could not be blown. Chicle was also unsuitable, proving too sticky to be used effectively as a base for bubble gum. It fell to Fleer to experiment with synthetic gum bases suitable for making bubbles, and his experiments lasted more than two decades. Finally, in 1906, Fleer marketed the first commercial bubble gum, which he named "Blibber-Blubber."

Despite the facts, that consumers could chew the new gum, that it tasted reasonably good, and that it could produce bubbles, the Fleer factory had not solved the conundrum of how to make a successful bubble gum. Blibber-Blubber stuck to the face, and it had to be removed using turpentine, not a process welcomed in most households. However, the Fleer company counted among its employees a young accountant, Walter Diemer, who eventually produced a usable bubble gum mix in early August 1928, in front of a crowded office. This was the turning point that was to revolutionize kids' appetites for several generations. The young man also hit on another innovation in food technology. He discovered how to add pink food coloring to the gray bubble gum mixture, and overnight he produced one of the sales sensations of the interwar years: a pink bubble gum that exploded in the face without damaging anybody—including the person who had blown the bubble.

The commercial implications of the invention of bubble gum were significant in ways that were not even guessed at in the 1930s. Bubble gum could be made successfully only from a synthetic gum base and, although exports of chicle continued to dominate the production process for chewing gum, the development of synthetics was eventually to shift the balance against the chicle producers. Chewing gum today is made from vinyl resins or microcrystalline waxes, producing a synthetic rubberlike substance similar to that used for the cover of golf balls. The dependence on chicle is long past. However, chicle had other qualities that were to lower its usefulness once synthetics began to appear. Chicle was a natural product and, like the Siamese jelutong base with which it was mixed, it was difficult to clean and could easily become contaminated. In the 1920s it was not uncommon to find insects in chewing gum made from chicle. The positive qualities that chicle did possess, and that were difficult to replicate synthetically, included excellent spring-back qualities for chewing. It was these that would eventually ensure that chicle became an ingredient in high-quality gums in our era of natural, organic products.

The invention of bubble gum and its commercial development in the 1930s and 1940s widened the appeal of the product, and clever marketing associated it with the icons of mass consumption in America at the time. Even before 1941, chewing gum had become associated with most of the key elements in American popular culture and myth: the movies, millionaires, national heroes, and sports. The bubble gum cards that accompanied gum in the 1930s featured heroes of the United States, battles, and national monuments.[3] J. Warren Bowman first marketed these, but other companies, including the Goudey Company of Boston and National Chicle of Cambridge, Massachusetts, all introduced cards with their gum during the 1930s, making bubble gum cards a household item. In particular, gum packets, like cigarettes, often contained baseball cards, and collectors were encouraged to build up teams and to swap players. In playgrounds all over the United States, and later in Europe, kids spent much of their leisure time collecting pictures of their sports idols and chewing as much gum as it required to build up a formidable collection.

The success of gum as a cultural product lay in its ambivalence. At one and the same time, it was harmless and yet it served to undermine authority. It was healthy, at least compared with alcohol or tobacco, but chewing gum also came to be seen as a manifestation of self-confidence and eventually of "cool." There were so few intrinsic qualities to gum that developing extrinsic ones became a competitive industry: In fact, chewing gum demonstrated anything the consumer wanted it to demonstrate. After America entered the war in 1941 and troops were issued gum as a part of their ration, developing extrinsic qualities even extended to rebranding gum as part of the national war effort.

War usually makes unusual demands on the civilian populations—as well as the forces—demands that are unlikely to be made in peacetime. Families are forced apart, everyday routines are changed or forgotten, and working roles are transformed, notably between the sexes. The movies and other medium of entertainment and communication, which play an important role in people's everyday lives, are transformed by war into avenues of escape or imagination. Looking at the history of chewing gum, it is not difficult to appreciate how the transformative effects of war played out for an everyday product that people took with them—into the armaments factories and cinemas, as well as the battlefields.

Chewing Gum Wars

Chewing gum had been associated with the armed forces even before it came into commercial use. Santa Anna's soldiers used chicle, as did the indigenous Maya, who were constantly involved in warlike activity for several centuries before the Spanish invasion. However, the first large-scale use of gum by combatants in modern times was in World War I. The U.S. military discovered that chewing gum freshened the mouth when toothbrushes and paste were not available and that it helped to quench thirst. It also was suggested that chewing gum helped to calm the nerves of combatants under fire. In 1918 the American Red Cross had shipped 4.5 million packs of chewing gum to France, and service personnel there used it when it was feared the retreating German army had poisoned the water. When the military engagement ended, and the troops returned home, large orders for gum were placed with American companies by Belgium, France, Italy, and the United Kingdom. This was the beginning of a process through which gum reached into the civilian market in continental Europe.

During World War II the inclusion of chewing gum in the military ration meant that consumption increased sixfold on prewar levels. American servicemen and women for the remaining years of the conflict consumed an average of 630 sticks of gum each year. American companies manufactured and shipped 150 billion sticks of gum to the forces serving overseas between 1941 and the end of hostilities in 1945.

The war also caused serious shortages of Siamese jelutong, which was mixed with chicle in many chewing gums and had been sourced from an area now occupied by the Japanese army. However, the other major ingredients of gum were also difficult to find—sugar was scarce in wartime, and it accounted for 60 percent of chewing gum's contents. Similarly, peppermint and spearmint, which flavored most chewing gum, were rationed. In addition, the U.S. manufacturers claimed that during the war their supplies of chicle from Mexico and Central America had dried up (a claim that is examined below).

The response of the Wrigley's company to the wartime shortages was to turn this disadvantage into a public relations exercise, by demonstrating that their gum was helping the war effort. Philip Wrigley feared that supply problems would force him to produce inferior-quality gum, which might undermine the company's long-term viability. At the same time, there was publicity to be derived from association with the forces' struggle for freedom overseas.

The solution was to withdraw all the familiar brands from the domestic market and to introduce a new brand, called Orbit, as "a plain but honest wartime chewing gum." Wrigley's produced billboards showing an empty wrapper of Wrigley's Spearmint gum, with the line "Remember this wrapper!" The advertising campaign worked, and even Orbit sold very well, although by 1945 supplies of the raw materials became so scarce that Philip Wrigley stopped production of every gum except Orbit. These shortages also gave a huge fillip to the development of synthetics, a process intensified five years later by the outbreak of the Korean War.

After 1946, when supplies gradually returned to normal, the consumption of chewing gum on the U.S. domestic market reached unprecedented heights. This was largely because of the important role chewing gum played within the wartime ration. It led to the dissemination of American gum to countries in Asia and Europe with serving U.S. military. In fact, however, many of these countries had developed markets for gum even before the war.

Wrigley had realized early on that Asia represented an important potential market for chewing gum. In 1913 he had traveled to

Asia in an effort to launch chewing gum there. He noted that in India chewing was deeply embedded cultural practice, but people chewed betel nuts, the fruit from a native plant, rather than anything that resembled chicle-based gum. Several thousand dollars were spent on a campaign to launch chewing gum in India, but it proved unsuccessful. However, this campaign was modest compared with the commercial onslaught on Japan that Wrigley's undertook in the early 1930s. The problem in Japan was that customers often swallowed the gum after chewing it, so Wrigley hired students to give lectures on how to chew and dispose of gum. They traveled between villages in rural Japan accompanied by a brass band and banner-waving peasants. When a crowd gathered, the students would hold up a stick of gum, unwrap it, and then chew it in front of the gathered crowd. Billboards appeared all over Tokyo, and during baseball games scoreboards explained what chewing gum was.

The critical problem in launching chewing gum in Asia, even before the outbreak of global hostilities in 1941, was that most people in the 1930s did not earn enough to buy it. This was first evident in Japan. But Wrigley hit on a solution to the problem of the limited spending capacity of average customers. In marketing gum to the Chinese, Wrigley allowed shopkeepers to open the packages and cut each stick in two. For one sen, Chinese consumers could buy one of these half sticks. In addition, Wrigley wrote informational bulletins on the virtues of gum, which were distributed in the countryside. The culturally grounded Chinese suspicion of billboards that combined a design with the printed word closed that as a marketing option, though. By 1935, two years before the Japanese army invaded, the Wrigley's company was selling more than a million dollars' worth of gum in China.

However, because of Wrigley's early successes in selling to Japan, the invasion prompted the Chinese to ban all Japanese goods (a category that included the American chewing gum), so the market quickly evaporated.

In the early 1930s Warren Bowman, another American bubble gum entrepreneur, was the first person to build bubble gum factories in Japan. Bowman was a large man in every respect: well over six feet tall and with a powerful ego to go with it. When people met him for the first time they were alarmed by his loud, booming voice and his evident pleasure in selling almost anything to anybody. Bowman was one of nature's entrepreneurs and was at his happiest when he had spotted a good sales pitch. On one occasion he even sold automobiles off the street to unsuspecting passersby.

William Wrigley had been one of Warren Bowman's heroes. Inspired by Wrigley's success, Bowman traveled to Chicago to view the famous Wrigley's skyscraper there. According to one account, his admiration for Wrigely's was such that he attracted attention to himself by spending so much time on the sidewalk gazing up at the Wrigley's building.[4] At this time he had only a few dollars to his name, but he managed to borrow enough to set himself up, with a few old machines, as the Bowman Chewing Gum Company. But he managed to lever several hundred more from a bank and soon went into business with some old machines and barrels of sugar and glucose, founding the Bowman Chewing Gum Company. He produced bubble gum brands that outsold most of his competitors, notably Blony and Bub, and introduced chewing gum cards into the packets. Originally these cards featured scenes with cowboys and Indians. However, he also introduced something more in keeping with gum's bellicose past—a 240-card series picturing war heroes and famous battles. Sales of the "Horrors of War" series produced by Bowman exceeded $100 million.

Bowman's gum did not meet the approval of teachers and parents, although it did find support from Japanese kids. They chewed it and spat it out until the authorities intervened to try to curb the habit. Officials condemned it as "injurious to public health" and the police in Japan were instructed to arrest perpetrators. But the real problem arose with the cards that accompanied Bowman's gum. The Japanese had recently invaded Manchuria in China and committed atrocities, some of which were highlighted in the cards. Not surprisingly, in 1937 the Japanese embassy officials in Washington protested to the U.S. State Department. They argued that Japan was a peace-loving country and insisted that Bowman withdraw his cards and gum from sale.

The State Department refused to acquiesce in the face of the Japanese protests. It argued that the Japanese government had just sunk a U.S. gunboat on the Yangtze River, one of the events depicted on Bowman's cards. Eventually the Japanese embassy withdrew its complaint, declared Bowman "an enemy of Japan," and instructed him to cease production in Japan.

Chewing Gum and the Ration

American military rations had developed during the Revolutionary War as a garrison ration, consisting mainly of meat and bread with some vegetables when in season. This ration was designed to serve the garrison en masse, although many soldiers made their own cooking arrangements. The purpose of the ration, originally established by resolution of Congress, was to improve the diet of soldiers. The intention was that, although animals were driven into camp, the preparation of food should not be entirely dependent on what livestock was available locally.

The military ration subsequently came to reflect a pared-down version of the real privations of diet on the frontier. It was simple, but it kept body and soul together. By the beginning of the nineteenth century, the ration included supplementary items, of which the most welcome were "spirits."[5] In October 1832 President Andrew Jackson substituted coffee and sugar for rum and brandy in an attempt to reduce alcoholism among the troops. By the time of the Civil War, however, the principle that military rations needed to be accepted by soldiers themselves was given fuller recognition. Not only coffee extract but also preserved meat and desiccated vegetables were procured for the forces because they were generally inexpensive and acceptable to the men. Preserved food varied widely in quality, and canned food, in particular, was often defective and unusable. The army had not cracked the major challenge of a military diet—how to provide food that the soldiers liked but in a form that was easy to carry and convenient to use.

During the Indian campaigns of 1865–1890, the military rations were invariably monotonous, unpalatable, and even inedible. The absence of fresh fruit and vegetables produced scurvy in the troops and also led some garrisons to grow their own fresh produce in makeshift gardens. Increasingly storage became an issue and, as so many of the soldiers were on the move at any given time, efforts were made to provide food that could be reconstituted, including dried vegetables and pemmican (originally derived from shredded buffalo meat). Jerked beef was another Indian item adopted for army use on the frontier during this period. It did little to prevent high mortality rates caused by poor diet and nutrition—fourteen soldiers died from illness and disease for every one who died from battle wounds.[6]

After 1901 the idea developed that service rations should be linked to the special duties performed by army personnel, whether they were in garrisons, on active service in the field, traveling or marching to a conflict, or fighting under emergency conditions. The ration increasingly featured items that soldiers enjoyed eating or drinking, such as corned beef, baked beans, and tomatoes. By World War I the accent was on rations that could be supplied to a mass army fighting in the field at a great distance from suppliers for the first time requiring close collaboration between the food industry and the food supply services of the military establishment. This was the period in which the production, distribution, and storage of food began to be taken seriously as an essential adjunct to war. The beginning of the twentieth century was also a time in which the food industry was being subjected to technological transformation, especially through canning, preserving, and freezing food.[7]

During World War I an emergency ration had been introduced that contained several items intended to lift morale as well as nourish the soldier. Foremost among these were three one-ounce chocolate bars, which soldiers liked, were easily packaged, and stored well. By 1920 soluble coffee was introduced, as well as soluble drinking chocolate. Within twenty years the ration included a series of essential foods with what we would today recognize as "feel-good" factor—twelve-ounce bars of bitter chocolate, sugar, and peanut butter, for example. By June 1940 the army had introduced the celebrated Logan Bar, named after its developer, Colonel Paul Logan. These bars became a part of the basic combat ration and entered most of the various assortments of food items packaged for American troops. Although palatable, these experimental bars had poor keeping qualities and, even more seriously, tended to induce thirst rather than reduce it. Combating thirst had always been one of the key objectives of armies fighting far from reliable supplies of liquid drinks.

In August 1941 the first large-scale procurement of materials for the service ration of World War II took place—1.5 million service rations, ready for American troops who could not access field kitchens. The idea was to produce a pack that could meet the daily needs of soldiers who were cut off from regular food supply and that needed little storage and shipping space. The new rations went beyond existing commercial practice in protecting packaged foods on the long journey from American factories to theaters of war. Shortages of some ingredients meant that the ration was a product of necessity rather than choice. Despite these difficulties, between 1941 and 1945 more than 1 billion special rations were procured at a cost of nearly $700 million.

It was at this point that chewing gum made a strategically important appearance in the wartime ration of the American GI. The C ration included an accessory pack, which was initially viewed as a supplement to the serious ingredients in the ration, like corned beef and dried vegetables. It included nine good commercial-quality cigarettes, water-purification tablets, matches, toilet paper, a can opener, and chewing gum. Other items, such as hard candy and candy-coated peanuts and raisins, were found to keep poorly and were abandoned. The accessory pack was divided into two packets—the long (accessory) pack and the short (cigarette) pack. Chewing gum, together with toilet paper, a can opener, salt, and a wooden spoon, were included in the long pack.

Subsequent army rations all made use of chewing gum, and the subsequent success of the ration, with attendant publicity, amazed those who had developed it at the time.[8] Chewing gum soon became part of every pack, sharing space with a canned meat product, biscuits, cigarettes, and a fruit bar in the breakfast pack; with canned cheese and cigarettes for dinner; and again with bouillon powder in the supper pack. The biscuits, beverages, fruit bars, and gum were packaged in a laminated cellophane bag, while the canned meat and cheese were put in a chipboard sleeve-type box. The two units were assembled and sealed in a waxed carton bearing the insignia of the K ration.

The success of chewing gum as an integral part of the American forces' ration became clear when the American forces had to carry their supplies with them into combat, especially during the Pacific War. A lightweight, concentrated pack had to include food that was already prepared, that the troops enjoyed, and that could be packed inside waterproof boxes during amphibious campaigns and assault landings. The contents needed to be unaffected by temperature and humidity, easily opened, stable for long periods of time, and appetizing. The classic "Assault Lunch," introduced in 1944 and in which chewing gum was an integral component, met all these demands. Intriguingly, an added complication was added to the pack: For reasons of secrecy none of the individual items could be labeled. Chewing gum was now an essential food item and a military secret.

In the early days of the war, pilots, crewmen, and passengers carried food items that they supplied themselves, including fruits and chewing gum. In 1943 their popularity was such that this "American" candy supplement was issued to U.S. fliers stationed in the United Kingdom. This supplement then became the basis

for the Air Forces Pocket Lunch and the Aircrew Lunch, which
later made its debut in September 1944. When an assessment was
made of the various rations after the war, it was concluded that
"The chewing gum, chocolate and hard candy included in the
flight lunch, were the only items considered desirable."[9] Different
versions of this pack adapted these key ingredients in different
ways: parachute landings for stowing in lifeboats, or for fitting in
the emergency vest pocket of air force personnel. In life-raft packs,
six B-complex vitamin tablets supplemented the chewing gum,
ensuring that gum helped provide the refreshment necessary in
the absence of fresh water supplies. Indeed, by the end of the war
chewing gum had found its way into the most essential items for
military survival. The perception of gum being considered frivo-
lous or nonessential in peacetime was transformed by the context
in which it was regularly consumed and enjoyed in wartime.

"Got Any Gum, Chum?"

Toward the end of World War I more than 1 million American
servicemen had visited the United Kingdom. Most of these troops
spent no more than a couple of weeks in England, as their visits
only marked a stopping point between the United States and the
battlefront in Flanders. In World War II it was very different.
Between 1942 and 1945, forty of the eighty-nine U.S. combat
divisions were stationed in the United Kingdom at one time or
an other. In total, more than 3 million American forces were
stationed in the United Kingdom during World War II—more than
one-quarter of all American troops serving overseas. On the eve of
D day, the numbers resident increased to 1.65 million, and even at

the end of the war there were still more than four hundred thousand American troops remaining in England. Much of this occupation was geographically concentrated, especially in London and the few major locations of American barracks. Although few American service personnel spent long periods in England, many spent from six to eight months in some part of the British Isles.[10]

The impact of this large-scale occupation was very mixed. Many ordinary British households never met an American serviceman, and relatively few welcomed them into their homes. Nevertheless, the sheer volume of Americans stationed in many parts of Britain had consequences for the way that British people perceived the United States. David Reynolds quoted a BBC research report in February 1944:

> Two years ago the sight of an American soldier anywhere in the country would have been a source of immediate comment and interest; today the United States uniform is, in many parts of Great Britain, as familiar as, if not more familiar, than our own.[11]

Millions of British people met an American for the first time in the years between 1942 and 1945. What had previously been seen as a former colony of the British—a *cousin* in family terms—was now seen as a foreign country with a very different culture and modes of behavior. Particularly among the young, first contact with Americans produced an unmistakable interest in all things American: Hollywood glamor, dance bands, and movie icons.[12]

Reynolds, in his fascinating study of the American occupation of Britain in wartime, argued that to make sense of the American presence, British citizens needed to relate it to other prewar and wartime points of contact. Most British families had no idea, for example, that American servicemen lived much better in the wartime army than in prewar, depression America. Indeed, most GIs in Europe, notwithstanding their youth, had come from families that had suffered much more from the Depression than did British families in Britain. The war served to transform the expectations and lives of American soldiers even more radically than that of the populations on which they were billeted.

Personal contact with the American forces merely underlined the cultural status of the United States, adding detail to, and elaborating upon, the global pretensions of the American Dream since the 1920s. By the 1940s, America had become the acme of modernity for many British people, particularly the young and less educated. By comparison, among the older and better educated people, the opposition to most things American was often intense and unyielding. G. M. Trevelyan, the revered British historian, bemoaned the fact that this was an age of no real culture except that of the Americans; real democracy had made an entry in the twentieth century through two world wars, and this had served "to cook the goose of civilization."[13] This analysis fell on deaf ears as far as most Britons were concerned, however:

> To those who loved American music and movies, the age of mass culture was a delight. The GIs—jitterbugging and gum-chewing—accentuated a trend that began during the Jazz Age of the 1920s and continued on via the gyrations of Elvis Presley to the present day.[14]

The contact with American culture, which before the war had been at best vicarious, now served to divide the British public. What they experienced was a precursor of the longer term process, in which *American* came to be synonymous with *global*. Unpacking the longer term effects of the "Americanization" of

Britain is difficult because Britain changed so rapidly during the period of the "American invasion." The American GI in Britain was the harbinger of different attitudes toward sex, enjoyed a radically different diet to that of native Britons at the time, and demonstrated a confident familiarity with mass culture as well as an unwillingness to be socially deferential. In the context of the chewing gum story, each of these elements is important: sex, food, and attitude.

The conventional view of the American occupation of Great Britain during World War II is that the average GI was "oversexed, overpaid, overfed, and over here." What is less often appreciated is that, so far as the British were concerned, the GIs were unconscious ambassadors for all that was appealing about American culture. Shifts in sexual behavior were signaled by the American presence—but not simply because the GI was "over-sexed." The evidence from interviews, news reports and Mass Observation surveys at the time suggested two additional explanations—they were shown enormous attention by a following of females, some of them girls too young to do war work, and others looking for the proverbial good time. They were also good news to the prostitutes of Piccadilly Circus and Shepherd Market in London's West End.

At the same time, the British were bored to death with the privations of the wartime siege economy, its monotonous diet of ration books, and regulations. The American presence reminded the British, or even introduced them to the idea, that there were goods to consume and parties to be had. Wartime Britain was a country not simply of promiscuous American soldiers but also of predatory women and unruly teenagers, many of whose parents were simply out of sight and mind.[15] For many British girls, a "Yank" "was someone encountered hitherto only on the cinema screen" and therefore surrounded by an aura that was impossible to dispel.

The GI, in turn, was very much better paid than his British counterpart. He earned a net disposable pay of about $40 a month in 1942, much of which was often spent on a one-day pass to the delights of London. The British soldier, by comparison, lived on about half this sum until 1944, and very little of it was disposable, coming in the form of allowances for his wife and children. To most GIs, life on the base was not that comfortable, but the relatively large disposable income could be spent on leisure and entertainment, not to mention the resources of a well-stocked post exchange. The British who befriended American troops were the indirect beneficiaries of this largesse, receiving gifts of chocolate, cigarettes, and the coveted nylons that were beyond the reach of British families.

Much of the attention lavished on GIs came from kids. The expected response to the catchphrase "Got any gum, chum?" from British kids was "Gotta sister, mister?" from the American serviceman. The simple pleasures of what the British called sweets, or candy, were denied to a generation of children by wartime rationing (which continued, in the case of candy, until 1951). Whether or not British kids asked for sweets and gum, they got it from the GIs, who organized parties for local children, particularly at Thanksgiving and Christmas. In just over two years, from 1942 to 1944, American air force units alone gave almost four hundred parties for more than fifty-eight thousand British kids.

Inevitably, the existence of so much plenty in a world of comparative poverty brought some unwanted responses on both sides. Reynolds noted that "for some GIs, handing out gum became little more than an amusing ritual (but) others got peeved at the amount of 'begging' they encountered," angry or irritated by the Britons' tendency to see all Americans as rich and ready to be fleeced. Gum, like other small but important pleasures, served to emphasize the differences between a country whose civilian population was bearing the brunt of the war and one that was not.

The impact of the American military presence was all the greater because, like Elvis Presley in the 1950s, some GIs were literally men from the movies:

> It was an open secret that Clark Gable—Rhett Butler of *Gone with the Wind*—was on an air base near Peterborough in the spring of 1943 (making a training film for gunners). James Stewart arrived in Norfolk in November 1943 and stayed until VE Day, first flying Liberators and then working as a staff officer. Glenn Miller, also in the U.S. Army, toured all over England from his base in Bedford until killed in an air crash in December 1944.[16]

It should be remembered that "going to the pictures" (i.e., the movies) was the most popular activity in England at this time. Cinema admissions rose from one billion a year in 1940 to about one and a half billion a year after 1942—which was equivalent to almost forty cinema visits for each member of the British population. What people saw on the screens was often a version of the American way of life, romanticized and sanitized, but in which people also were able to exercise personal freedom to consume what they wanted. Against the backdrop of an ordered, uptight British society in which everybody knew their place and learned to behave properly without apparently winning any great prizes, the

Hollywood world must have seemed excessive and unimaginably seductive. It was urbane and sophisticated and, several decades later, would be referred to with the epithet *cool.*

To the British, all things American were glamorous and full of temptation, providing valuable lessons in directness and equality for a class-ridden society in which social niceties separated the population—both civilian and within the armed forces. British wartime movies often depicted the officer class in a pastiche of upper-class revelry—enjoying their privileged freedom to do and say what they thought, while the ranks were usually treated as comic film extras because they were working class. American popular culture enabled the British to reexamine their social categories, and to aspire to a society in which anybody could, in principle, obtain anything.

Postwar Markets for Gum

The end of hostilities brought a boom to the domestic market for chewing gum in the United States, and within a few years postwar consumption leaped by more than 500 percent. Chicle was now easily available from the Yucatán and Central America, and trade routes to Asia were restored for American companies. In 1946 Andrew J. Paris from Texas was featured on the cover of *Life* magazine; having imported five thousand tons of chicle from Mexico, he was hailed as a national hero for America's kids. And wartime had definitely not suppressed home demand. It had actually given it a deferred boost by associating gum with the war effort. Chewing gum had acquired greater respectability in the postwar world. During wartime, a "pink market" had developed in the

United States as kids hoarded gum and sold it for up to one dollar a piece, keeping it fresh overnight in water. Chewing gum had acquired the aura of a strategic good and had come to represent America in an intangible way.

Chewing Gum Rations: The Fallout in Mexico

In the United States it had been argued that chewing gum was removed from the domestic market because suppliers could not keep up with the requirements of the draft. From Mexico the situation looked rather different—a product, which appeared to be important to the American war effort, was being bought for prices so low that they kept most chicleros at poverty levels. The final curtain came when it was realized that chicle had an uncertain future in the face of competition from the new synthetic gums that had been first developed for the bubble gum market. The development of synthetic gums, which wartime conditions had accelerated, eventually sounded the death knell for large-scale chicle production on the prewar model.

In June 1943 representatives of chicle cooperatives traveled to the United States to "discuss and defend the price of chicle, which is one of the most appreciated wartime materials in the United States."[17] Mexican producers claimed that the price they received was far too low, and they wanted to be paid in gold coins rather than in dollars. At this time the three major importers were Beech Nut of New Jersey, William Wrigley's of Chicago, and the American Chicle Company of New York. Between them, in 1942, these companies imported nearly 4 million kilos of chicle from Mexico.

The strategic importance of chicle during the war, together with the triumph of President Cardenas's brand of left, nationalist politics, had brought the demands of the Mexican chicle industry out into the open. The Mexican state began to intervene in the chicle industry, seeking to bring exports under government control and to secure better prices for the chicle cooperatives by regulating supply through the Banco National de Comercio Exterior (External Development Bank) and the Ministry of Agriculture. Using cooperatives as the vanguard of state regulation, Mexico began to protect the industry in the face of declining prices (by the end of the 1940s) and competition from both other producer countries and the new synthetics.

The socialization of the chicle industry during the 1940s and 1950s did nothing to hide its parlous state. Indeed, it was one of the reasons that state intervention was so intense. Of the forty chicle cooperatives created in the 1930s under Cardenas, only half survived to 1955. In 1956 and 1957 a new political movement came into being which sought to bring chicleros together and to increase the amount they received from $6.50 to $9.50 a kilo. In 1964 a Commission for Forestry and Chicle was created under Governor Rufo Figueroa, but again, the commission served only to underline the problems faced by the industry and did little to ameliorate the adverse social effects of the industry's decline.

The extent to which Mexico's chicle industry was now controlled by the state can be seen from the way in which production cooperatives dominated the industry, although their numbers had declined considerably. By 1978 there were only four leading private producers, while forty-six cooperatives were dedicated to chicle production and marketing. The difficulties for a government that wished to defend the chicleros lay in the structure of the industry. In the 1950s Wrigley's was the biggest buyer of chicle, and much of the rest of production was illegal—the contraband trade via Belize was still buoyant and probably represented about one-fifth of Mexico's exports.[18]

The decline set in, and the industry's principal market, the United States, never returned to full strength after the boom years of the 1940s. However, by the early 1990s new markets had begun to develop in Asia, particularly in Japan and Korea, where the demand for natural chicle was high. By 1993 these exports to the Far East represented one-fifth of the income from Mexico's forest products.

During the 1990s chicle production witnessed a minirevival, prompted by the new interest in natural forest products and sustainable forest management. The heavy costs of collecting chicle and the widespread destruction of the tropical forests had, since the 1940s, damaged much of Yucatán's chicle industry. What remained was increasingly concentrated in more remote areas, such as Calakmul on the border with Guatemala, where chicleros were organized in cooperatives whose main expressed goal was forest conservation and sustainable management. By the turn of the twenty-first century the chicle industry had to be located within a new set of developmental parameters, including common property resource management and longer-term forest conservation. In March 1998 there were still more than one thousand producers, largely organized within cooperatives, working in Mexico. As we see in chapter 7, the areas in which chicle had traditionally been tapped were now the scene of a new unfolding drama, as hundreds of thousands of tourists from Europe and North America converged on the Caribbean coast.

Places like Akumal, Cozumel, and Tulum were the heartlands of chicle, but by the end of the twentieth century they were the playgrounds of mass tourism. By the turn of the new century these same places yielded a new profit based on their beaches and reefs—the financial rewards of global tourism. The memory of chicle, once the single most important commercial activity in the zone, was confined to older people, many of them still living deep within the forest. And because of the brutality of everyday life experienced by chicleros, it was a memory every bit as sad as it was proud. However, the history of chicle extraction did not quite end there—as we see in the final chapter, there has been a resurrection of interest in chicle and its role in the chewing gum story. Today not only do the forests of Quintana Roo provide the backcloth for a more sustainable forest product but the international tourists who vacation on the Mexican Caribbean are offered an ersatz experience of chicle. Another avenue for mass consumption and popular taste has opened up.

MASS CONSUMPTION
AND POPULAR TASTE

Nicole was the product of much ingenuity and toil. For her sake trains began their run at Chicago and traversed the round belly of the continent to California; chicle factories fumed and link belts grew link by link in factories; men mixed toothpaste in vats and drew mouth-wash out of copper hogsheads; girls canned tomatoes quickly in August or worked rudely at the Five-and-Tens on Christmas Eve; half-breed Indians toiled on Brazilian coffee plantations and dreamers were muscled out of patent rights in new tractors—these were some of the people who gave a tithe to Nicole, and as the whole system swayed and thundered onward it lent a feverish bloom to such processes of hers as wholesale buying, like the flush of a fireman's face holding his post before a spreading blaze.[1]

F. Scott Fitzgerald, *Tender Is the Night* **(1934)**

During most of the nineteenth century rich American men went to Paris and Florence to purchase works of art. Their daughters and wives bought the season's haute couture on the fashionable streets of Paris. The scholars who went to Harvard and Yale to study later left for universities in Germany and England. American heiresses of marriageable age visited England to meet young men of title and spent weekends at Edwardian country house parties. European tastes and values were copied from the upper echelons of European society and transported to the body politic of America's moneyed classes. In the vicinity of Central Park, New York, the streets were lined with mansions in the style of the English and Italian Renaissance, Georgian and the French Baroque. Art and culture in the United States, at least for the upper classes, was noticeably European and, by 1900, increasingly so.

A century later it was American culture that dominated the globe. By the year 2000, American movies, American media networks, the (American) World Wide Web, and American designer fashion labels had acquired all the kudos of European taste a hundred years earlier. People on the street, everywhere in the world, sported American baseball hats, wore American T-shirts, visited a McDonald's, and used American English in conversation. If they spoke English as a second language, which many of them did, then they tried to acquire an authentic American accent. Against the opposition of rival cultural systems, the American prevailed. And although many of the products that people consumed were increasingly made in Europe or the Far East, they were invariably modeled on something American and reflected American patterns of consumption and taste.

The history of chewing gum is, at one level, an example of the globalization of taste; at another level it can be explained as the outcome of Americanization. Nicole's consumption, in the passage from F. Scott Fitzgerald's novel with which this chapter opened, made many things move and shake, among them the chicle factories of the American city. As this book has demonstrated, behind these factories lay an even more invisible process, that of chicle tapping and the colonization of the tropical forests of Yucatán.

Chewing Gum and Popular Culture

The development of mass consumption in early-twentieth-century America was linked, as we have seen, to the economic and demographic growth of American society, especially rapid urbanization and migration to the cities. Although popular culture existed before the age of mass consumption, its evolution and preeminence over high culture required that the Gordian knot with European culture be cut.

The primary influence of Europe on American taste and culture was to change radically in the next twenty years. The congregation of large numbers of people in cities and in factories in late-nineteenth-century America made the traditional entertainments of rural society impossible. What arose from within American society were forms of recreation and spectator sports that, while they owed something to England, were essentially made in America. P. T. Barnum brought the circus to the cities and made it a popular entertainment on a scale hitherto unknown, using three acres of circus tent and hundreds of extras.

This upheaval in popular recreation was made possible by technology but was not determined by it. As David Nye argued, national cultures were less technologically *determined* than technologically *determining*.[2] Partly through much improved transportation and better business methods, urban America was embarking on a revolution in popular expectations.[3] In time, it became the font of both mass entertainments and popular spectator sports.

By incorporating forms of expression and creating identities for people in their everyday lives of work and leisure, popular culture was to prove both *less* than the traditional liberal arts and at the same time *more* than them. But before mass consumption could renew and transform popular culture, the production of commodities for the mass market had to take precedence over all other forms of production. In turn it drove a wedge between the labor of the workshop and the artifact of the laborer.

Thenceforth it was the product, the commodity, that received attention from the society and that had value, rather than the relationship with the person or persons who produced it. One of the most important facets of commodity production, then, was that after 1914 it increasingly served to displace labor from the picture.[4]

Labor and production relations often had been invisible in the past, of course, but before the early twentieth century most of those who labored were destined to consume very little. The new century, and the American continent, changed all that. The era of mass production was also one of mass consumption, and it should hardly come as a surprise to find that many of the new products that were consumed became invested with meaning and importance by the new consuming classes.[5]

Chewing gum became widely available in American society at a time when work itself was being reformulated and workers were challenged to accept a level of multitasking that had few precedents in urban society. Chewing gum was a continuous activity and, like the production line for Model T Fords, it did not require a worker to break off from his or her activity. The difference was that gum spelled enjoyment. The workers who chewed gum often ate snack food as well, but chewing gum often was consumed as a substitute for food, as well as a complement. It filled a new space in the landscape of consumption by fitting in with the demands of peoples' lives. The cultural importance of gum was linked to its plasticity; it was illustrative of the change in labor relations and the patterns of consumption that facilitated these changes.

Another key element in this evolving process was the way that raw materials could be sourced from geographically remote areas that were essential for new commodities. By 1918 sourcing from such areas was easier than ever before, thanks to steamships, the telegraph, and refrigerated shipping. The distance between the raw materials for a product and the consumption of the product often made the producer almost invisible—as in the case of chicle. As with many food products, including chewing gum, the question few people considered was, Where on earth did this come from? New consumer products appeared with awesome regularity, on the table and in the shops. It is unlikely that many people stopped to think how they were made and whether their manufacture carried implications for other peoples' lives. Nicole, in F. Scott Fitzgerald's novel, gave little attention to the "chicle factories [that] fumed" and even less to the chicle tappers in Mexico, but the inexorable process that brought them together concluded with the "feverish bloom" that sent people away from shops as satisfied customers. The modern consumer inhabited a world of his or her own, blessed with the knowledge that they were oiling the wheels of capitalism.

Another aspect of chewing gum that requires some attention is that of the relationship between the source and the final product. It is clear that spatial scales do not exist independently of societies—they are socially produced and reproduced. The history of chewing gum provides evidence of the significance of spatial relations, particularly the way that spatial scales are linked to the evolution of capitalist economic relations.[6] The social and political struggles of rebel Maya and chicleros in the Yucatán, as well as those of chicle factory workers in the United States, make sense as part of these spatial relations. When it was difficult, and increasingly irrelevant, to source chewing gum from the tropical forests of Mexico and Central America, chewing gum was manufactured from other ingredients that could be made to order. The technological changes that made synthetic gum possible by the 1930s, spurred on by the development of the elusive bubble effect, held consequences for Mexican producers at a time when nationalism was reasserting itself south of the border. They illustrate the way in which social relations of production, and the livelihoods and communities they support, can suddenly become dispensable with shifts in demand. Although the connections between Nicole's shopping and the Yucatán seem tenuous, they nonetheless illustrate power relationships, embedded in geography.[7]

Spatial relationships are necessary to the commodity itself, to its production and consumption, but they are also necessary in another sense, since some products (and chewing gum is clearly one) achieve their iconic status from the fact that their origins cannot be easily identified. They serve to underline one of the most evident features of advanced capitalist markets. This feature is that popular taste can elevate a product, sometimes even making it a fetish and often providing strong cultural associations that serve to deepen the consumer's attachment to it. In this sense popular taste and mass consumption are complements to each other, and it is difficult to explain one without explaining the other. Wittgenstein referred to "the mystery of appearances as they unfold in front of us."[8] In chewing gum we witness not only the commercial invention of a product but also the evolution of popular culture through the product.

The history of gum, like many other popular consumer products, required the expansion of new consumer markets for a commodity that had previously eluded the market. In Mexico the itinerant workers who migrated to the forest frontier in the early twentieth century were part of a larger circle of transient labor in that country—and transient laborers in the United States were among those who consumed the gum. However, it was clear from the beginning of the century that power lay with the individuals who could harness natural resources and this itinerant labor to do business and make profits. The returns on chicle extraction often were spectacular for Mexican and foreign entrepreneurs, and the capital they accumulated was invested in the towns and cities of the United States. Commodity supply zones like those of the Yucatán Peninsula imply a particular vision of sociopolitical relations that appears both local and international to different groups of people—and both invisible and highly visible at the same time.[9]

Chicle is harvested from a tree that grows in the wild, and its intrinsic value is negligible. And until the trees become scarce (and thus valuable), they will continue to provide resin, almost as a "free good," such as rainwater or oxygen. What comes between this abundant supply and its manufacture, of course, is the labor of the chicleros. Increasingly, too, we recognize in the depletion of resources the real costs of not conserving them. Part of the appeal, and cultural importance of gum, lay in the fact that it represented something for nothing. But it was not free at the point of sale. Indeed, the backcloth to its production was replacing something that had been free in nature with something people bought. The value added to gum by its manufacture was taste, fashion, convenience, and brand.

In the case of the Yucatán, the boom years for chicle production facilitated the transformation of the environment by bringing the Mexican state to bear on what had hitherto been seen as a remote jungle region. Later, the gradual demise of the chicle economy provided another opportunity for the Mexican state to rework social relations in the zone. Having "Mexicanized" the frontier by suppressing the Mayan resistance in 1901, thirty years later, under President Cardenas, the Mexican state sought to socialize production. Chewing gum in the United States, the finished product, represented part of the repertoire of popular taste, while in Mexico (where popular culture was equally important) chicle stood for relations of dependency and subordination, if it was recognized at all.

In Mexico chicle held another kind of association, and one that fitted more conveniently into a picture of economic dependence. Chicle production, through the fragility of its dependence on international markets, epitomized a more vulnerable economic system. The chiclero's knowledge and pride in his craft passed into memory with little external social recognition, like that of other workers in primary production, such as miners or lumbermen. The chewing gum story in Mexico reveals a darker side of history, much of which has still received little public acknowledgment.[10]

The organization of space in the chewing gum world was dictated by the economic preeminence of the United States and the power of even ordinary consumers to influence development elsewhere. Its consumption by the new urban masses was necessarily linked to capital penetration in spatially remote areas whose very remoteness did nothing to prevent them from being transformed overnight. When the same consumer demands were freed from the geographical connections with Yucatán and could be met without the involvement of Mexican forest workers, business logic overwhelmed any other political or economic considerations. Chicleros were dumped on the scrap heap of history with even less ceremony than coal miners or shipyard workers, whose skills also became redundant.

This brings us to the third element in the complex relationship between popular taste and mass consumption in the history of chewing gum: the contested nature of globalization as the process responsible for linking a commodity with the world market. Today globalization is routinely celebrated or derided as the mechanism through which commodities and values are disseminated on the world scale:

> The stretching and deepening of social relations and institutions across space and time such that, on the one hand, day-to-day activities are increasingly influenced by events happening on the other side of the globe and, on the other hand, the practices and decisions of local groups can have significant global reverberations.[11]

In the case of chewing gum, mass consumption and popular taste have advanced with the process of globalization. Globalization and the mass production of a commodity are linked, through branding and advertising, in ways that affect the register of popular taste. Globalization clearly forces us to reconsider space and its relationship with power, as well as the limitations of territorial divisions in explaining the relations between societies.[12]

Several things remain clear in assessing the bigger picture into which the history of chewing gum falls. First, globalization does not mean the triumph of the universal over the particular. "The ways in which space and time are understood, and perhaps refashioned, are not universal," and we would be foolish to ignore the role of "local space within globalizing economies."[13] In the case of gum, as in other cases, local systems of production coexist with global brands and products. In Greece today there are more than twenty brands of chewing gum, mostly sourced from sprucelike resins, similar to what chicle replaced in late-nineteenth-century America. Chewing gum is about cultural difference in today's world as much as it is about uniformity.

Second, it is clear that whatever the cultural weight acquired by a product in the course of its life, there can be little question that it is historically dependent on the economic and power relations that brought the product to the market in the first place. Primary commodity supply zones, such as the Yucatán in this instance, often play a key role in the wider histories of consumption and taste. But the full significance of the commodities of specific cultures and social formations is constantly changing and being reconfigured. Chewing gum today is not the same commodity as it was in 1941, neither in its material composition nor in its cultural resonance. Patterns of mass consumption, together with popular taste, are capable of modification and adaptation to changing circumstances and economic conditions. We can only wonder at "the libidinous, performative and novelty-generating potentialities of social life."[14] These qualities also are found in commodities, which acquire and impart meanings from everyday life and then rework them every day.

Examples abound of social institutions that enable commodities to adapt to popular taste, facilitating different patterns of consumption, in different locations, by different groups of people. The history of tobacco furnishes examples of how a custom that was at first confined to white males spread to new smoking cultures and also provided opportunities for the penetration of new markets.[15] Another example is that of chocolate, which until World War I was known largely as a beverage but is now principally a confectionery item of global proportions.[16]

At some point, of course, chocolate was *cacao* (and "cocoa," the drink) rather than the confectionery bar we have grown to know and associate with specific global brands, like Nestlé, Cadbury, or Hershey. It was harvested from pods that grow on trees in the tropics. Similarly chicle needed to be transformed industrially into chewing gum before it could be marketed successfully in the United States and later on in the international market. The more that chicle became chewing gum, the more of a commodity it became, and the more it developed into a global product. Social relations in spatially distinct regions then became fully subordinated to the demands of global commodity production and the promotion of global brands. In the case of chewing gum, popular taste provided the impetus, through branding and imaginative marketing, for a global product, although in some cases the global marketing adventure failed.[17]

The centrality of taste, and the role it can play in mass consumption, is clear if we compare chewing gum with other products that might appear more important in a narrow economic sense, such as hydrocarbons or minerals, which also are traded on the global market. In these cases the possibility of scarcity of supplies, together with the need to consider pollution "sinks," has elevated their discussion to one of strategic necessity. Ensuring that these commodities can be bought is a premise of international economic survival, and often is the pretext for war. The idea of natural limits is invoked in these cases to bridge the gap between current levels of consumption and the expected consequences (or externalities) associated with them. Their strategic importance guarantees them a high-profile discourse.

In the case of gum there is no postscarcity discourse to inform our view of the importance of the resource.[18] Chewing gum illustrates the way in which nature is produced materially and discursively. Unlike the case, for example, of hydrocarbons, this is not primarily because discourse facilitates the acceptance (or rejection) of awkward political choices but because the commodity is itself discursively produced. Chewing gum cannot be separated from its associations and the desires it evokes. Without marketing and branding it is difficult to imagine commercial gum as a global commodity for which there is effective demand. The contrast with hydrocarbons could hardly be greater—even where we live is closely linked to the use we make of fossil fuels. Although originally sourced from nature, chewing gum illustrates the triumph of discourse over substance. Gum is chewed and spat out, and it exists for no other purpose than to satisfy bodily pleasure. It is one of the fullest realizations of an "embodied social life"—a life lived through the act of consumption itself.[19]

There are several ways in which chewing gum forces us to reflect on mass consumption and popular taste: as an exemplar and a test of theory. Chewing gum, like smoking or eating and drinking, is a primary bodily activity. It is associated with pleasure and contentment but also with denial (of food or liquids). Gum has acted as a substitute for what we do not have and, although usually represented as a synonym for enjoyment, has attracted little critical attention.

Within the history of its production, and transformation from a raw natural product into a commodity, chewing gum also reveals the fault lines that demarcate the United States from its neighbor to the south. In Mexico the production of chicle was briefly associated with political struggles over land and the resources it commands. But in this book I have argued that the materialization of chicle into gum has a wider and largely unacknowledged role in mass consumption and popular taste well beyond the frontiers of either Mexico or the United States. Through aggressive marketing and market opportunism, chewing gum has achieved universal status. I trust that I have demonstrated that chewing gum has a history of its own, and one that throws light on the societies from which it came.

At the same time, chewing gum is also part of who we are, not simply in the bodily sense that it is ingested (and egested) but also because it helps define who we are. It has achieved this powerful cultural identity by epitomizing all the things that go into making the individual human being interesting in the postscarcity age: a being capable of having attitude, of acting cool, of creating taste, and of freeing himself or herself from the strictures of brute necessity.

WHAT IT LEFT

BEHIND . . .

What *did* chewing gum leave behind? Much of the Yucatán Peninsula was transformed after the commercial decline of the chicle industry in the 1960s. Since then, the coast of Quintana Roo has developed as a global tourist destination, much of it branded as "The Mayan Riviera."[1] There is a history to this development, and an interesting one, but it does not necessarily help us answer the question that the story of chewing gum leads us to ask—Where has chicle left its mark? Is there a connection between the vestiges of chicle production and the way in which tourism has grown? If we trace the history of tourist pioneers in the area, we certainly discover that some of them were chicle contractors before they became interested in tourism.[2] Similarly, we can explore what has happened to the resources of Quintana Roo today, of which chicle was among the most

Playa del Carmen today

important, with reference to another parallel development—
that of global conservation and the creation of two major
biosphere reserves.[3] These reserves have attracted attention
from ecologists and scientists and increasingly take small parties of people into the protected areas in four-wheel drive
vehicles. Chicle was an important raw material before the
language of sustainable forestry had been invented. From
today's perspective, the harvesting of chicle resin might have a
real potential contribution to make to forest conservation as
part of an integrated system.

Finally, attempts are being made to combine elements of both
these strands—tourist development and conservation—in the
form of ecotourism or sustainable tourism, approaches for which
the region is already justifiably famous.[4] This has even led to
sporadic attempts to take tourists to visit disused chicle camps in
the forest and to establish arboretum that include the famed
chicozapote tree (which is now part of the flag of the state of
Quintana Roo). Along the coasts and jetties of the Mexican
Caribbean there is evidence of "zapote" wood having been
employed in construction, but today it is a protected species and
cannot be cut for commercial use.

These lines of inquiry, if employed together with documentary
evidence, can help us fully establish chewing gum's legacy in
Yucatán. To try to do that, we need to return to the historical
spaces that were closely associated with chicle and examine the
tangible evidence of the history described in this book. All the
principal sites for chicle have subsequently become part of the
roll call of tourist destinations on the coast, catering for both
mass and niche tourist markets—Cozumel, Akumal, Tulum,
Puerto Vallarta, Isla Mujeres, and many more.

Contemporary mural, which reads, "The Mayan Zone is not an ethnographic museum, but a people on the march"

The flag of the state of Quintana Roo
(with chicle and cross)

Restaurant named after chicle in Felipe Carrillo Puerto

Central Vallarta—The Abandoned Chicle Camp

A person traveling south of Cancún on the main coastal highway will soon reach the port of Puerto Vallarta. A port is exactly what it is, and today Puerto Vallarta has managed to avoid, or be excluded from, most of the tourist development that characterizes the Mexican Caribbean coast. There are docks and a busy trade in container freight, together with a few hotels and restaurants and a few modest shops. Tourists from Cancún arrive in hired cars for a taste of the best Mexican shellfish in an atmosphere less staged than that of Cancún, something more resembling a small Mexican town.

The roads out of Puerto Vallarta appear to run either north or south, but, in fact, across the main highway is a poorly surfaced track that runs inland, into what remains of the once impressive forest. Up this stony track about an hour away is an abandoned chicle camp, Central Vallarta, which was once the epicenter of trade in the area. Today almost nobody is there, since there is no village or significant Mayan population. What remains of the camp is contained in a few disused buildings, which when I visited were being protected by a lively Honduran migrant, Eliseo, who spent a lot of the time drinking beer, surrounded by empty bottles. Anyone who cares to take a look around the camp is given a tour by Eliseo, in return for a small cash donation, or booze.

Visiting Central Vallarta is rather like discovering the *Marie Celeste,* an abandoned ship in a calm ocean. The buildings are filled with rubble, but they also contain innumerable pieces of evidence of the chicle industry and its practitioners in the past. There are plenty of the little canvas sacks that chicleros used to carry the resin—brown, worn, and covered in gum—as well as

Deserted house used by chicleros in 1950s in Central Vallarta

the weights and measures that accompanied chicle production. There are old, battered *marquetas,* the brick-sized molds into which the chicle was poured before it was carried out of the forest on the backs of mules. In addition, there is all the detritus one might expect in a camp that has been abandoned for almost a half a century—old domestic equipment, cooking utensils, pots and pans. Whatever Central Vallarta is today, it is not a reconstruction of anything—it is not a piece of heritage tourism, although I was told some tourists do arrive in groups, as part of ecotourist trips into the interior, organized by an office in Puerto Vallarta. What remains to be seen is whether camps like this one can be refashioned as part of new ecotourist packages.

Cozumel—The Chewing Gum Entrepôt

The nineteenth-century archaeologists and surveyors John Stephens and Frederick Catherwood discovered Cozumel at the end of March 1841, during their expedition by boat in search of new Mayan ruins.[5] They sailed past Isla Mujeres, or "Mugeres" as Stephens dubbed it, which is an island notorious as the headquarters of a pirate called Lafitte (after whom a number of luxury hotels on the coast have now been named). Next was Cancún (or "Kancune" to Stephens), which left a poor impression on the travelers. It was nothing but "a barren strip of land, with sand hills, where the water was so salt we could barely drink it." Whenever they landed in search of fresh water they were pursued by hordes of "moschetoes" that made life very difficult (and would have continued to do so 130 years later if the Mexican government had not decided to spray the area).

They went on to land on the island of Cozumel at the only inhabited spot, the ranch of San Miguel. Here they stopped to feast on turtle and fresh water, strolled along the shoreline picking up shells, and slept in hammocks. (They were "as piratical a group as ever scuttled a ship at sea," reported Stephens to his diary.) The island of Cozumel had, of course, been discovered several times before, the first European being Juan de Grijalva in March 1518, who ended up lost at sea after leaving Cuba.

Soon after Stephens and Catherwood arrived, the island was the refuge for people fleeing the ravages of the Caste War on the mainland. These were the founders of Cozumel, as far as local people are concerned today, and a section of the town's museum is dedicated to the "true Mexicans" who came to the island and established businesses and a flourishing export trade in timber, fish, and chicle.

The Museum of Cozumel is well worth a visit for its celebration of an iconoclastic history. Many of the exhibits are dedicated to the early pioneers whose small businesses laid the basis for a more measured, sensitive tourist economy than that of Cancún. Some of these people opened restaurants and some hotels. The earliest hotels, the Grand Hotel Louvre, as well as the Hotels Yuri and Playa, were built in the 1930s and 1940s, but by 1970 there were many more after an explosion of hotel building. What makes Cozumel distinctive is that its citizens trace themselves back to the refugees who arrived in the late 1840s and regard the accomplishments of the Cozumel economy as directly attributable to their common sense and business acumen.

A significant amount of the capital for Cozumel's early tourism undoubtedly came from the trade in chicle. Martin Ramos Diaz recorded three meetings that were held between the representatives of Wrigley's and the rebel Maya in 1921, all of them on Cozumel.[6]

The key intermediary in these meetings was Juan Bautista Vega, a man originally from Cozumel who had been captured by the rebel Maya as a child on the mainland and brought up among them. The object of the meetings was to ensure that one of the most important chicle exporting companies, Negociacion Chiclera Mexicana, under the control of Carlos Pardio, could continue to have access to the rich chicle resources of Chumpon and Tulum despite the constant warfare between the indigenous Maya and the soldiers of the Mexican state. Cozumel, as an island deeply involved in the chicle trade, served as the perfect bridge between the mainland Maya and the chewing gum companies. That the Mexican state was still at war with the Mayan rebels did not prevent Wrigley's, or their agents, from traveling to the island to negotiate with them.

The Museum of Cozumel contains one exhibit dedicated to chicle. It represents a small camp in a *hato,* or clearing in the forest, and shows the daily life of the camp and the working tools and materials used by chicleros. In a sense, it simply took the camp at Central Vallarta, cleaned it up for inspection, and put it indoors in a museum.

Vigia Chico—Retracing the Chicle Railroad

Some things cannot be consigned to museums. One of them is the infrastructure associated with chicle. During the summer of 2002, I was staying near the coast of Quintana Roo in the town of Felipe Carrillo Puerto, the site of some of the fiercest Mayan resistance to the whites during the Caste War (where the rebel Maya founded their citadel, Chan Santa Cruz, as we saw in chapter 3). Felipe

Child in electric car in Felipe Carrillo Puerto

Chicozapote tree growing within a
Mayan nature reserve

Carrillo Puerto was also an important center for chicle production; the forests surrounding it were rich with chicozapote trees.

Today Felipe Carrillo Puerto is a quiet town outside the tourist loop, although it is eager to join the burgeoning tourist economy and impatient of its apparent exclusion. There are a few shops, a couple of hotels, and a number of ordinary restaurants catering to the passing commercial trade. It is halfway to the capital of the state, Chetumal, on the border with Belize. There is a Cruzoob church well away from the center of the town, and its adherents are tolerated, if not exactly feted, by the local inhabitants.

Felipe Carrillo Puerto is also home to a number of oppositional political groups: lawyers working on behalf of political factions, peasant leaders, and those working for the "disappeared." A newspaper is published in the Mayan language, and a small library and collection of traditional musical instruments can be found in a local house that serves as a museum. There is no museum dedicated to chicle. The much bigger Casa de Cultura contains a bookshop and art gallery and meeting rooms for local organizations. In a modest way this is an appropriate reworking of its past as the center of indigenous resistance, and it is a source of pride for local people. In the evenings, parents bring their small children to the main square where they drive little electric cars around the plaza and eat food from stalls and modest restaurants. It is a scene that could be repeated in hundreds, if not thousands, of Mexican towns.

Most people who enter Felipe Carrillo Puerto today are either intent on driving south, toward the much less developed parts of the coast, or through the Biosphere Reserve of Sian Khan to other, less populated areas that serve as meeting grounds for scuba divers and sport fishing. Those who are heading north are on their way to important Mayan sites like Coba and Tulum, both of which are now served by international hotels and have fully embraced global tourism.

The signposts at the center of town suggest another route, however, and one that is never taken by tourists or commercial travelers. This sign points toward Vigia Chico, and the road is a disincentive to anybody but the most persistent or foolhardy. It takes more than two hours to reach by four-wheel drive vehicle, up the stony track from Felipe Carrillo Puerto to the coast at Vigia Chico, through dense jungle and, eventually, mangroves. Tourists do not visit but prefer to stay in one of the comfortable bed and breakfast establishments at Punta Allen, across the bay, where brochures tell them about the history of the area and even mention the central part played by Vigia Chico in the chicle trade. Vigia Chico was the principal point through which chicle was exported, first to Cozumel and then to the United States. When General May returned to his people from Mexico City, having been lionized by President Carranza, he landed at Vigia Chico and was unable to convince his newly acquired girlfriend that she too was safe in the hands of the Mayan warriors waiting on the shore.

The road to Vigia Chico takes the same route as the railway line that had carried chicle to the boats and that was constantly attacked by Mayan snipers. It also had carried the governor of Yucatán, Siurob, to negotiate with General May in 1926, when the concession for the railway was being considered and General May was gradually being relieved of his powers. The railway had been built at great cost to human life. Mule-drawn platforms and steam locomotives had hauled narrow-gauge tracks from the port, and the line had been built slowly and painfully. The workers were prey to snakes and the sun, the prospect of malaria without medicines, and the attacks of the Mayan insurgents. As Nelson Reed put it, the "dynamite used to blast the road-head was a death knell to the still unreconstructed Maya, [and] the railroad spikes were nails in their coffin."[7]

Once one arrived at Vigia Chico in the 1920s or 1930s, the sight was less than edifying. I described it briefly in chapter 3.

> It was a collection of barracks, whorehouses, a clapboard hotel with a verandah, and miserable pens for convict labor along the beach, all centering on a pier of considerable dimensions. In spite of the railroad and telegraph line to Santa Cruz and visits from occasional ships, it was an isolated, hated place. The principal sight was the rusting hulk of the wrecked gunboat *Independencia.* The quality of life there is suggested by the presence of glass floors in several of the buildings, floors made by pushing rum bottles upside down into the sand.[8]

Today there are no glass floors, only a small military camp and a Mexican flag flying over the buildings. The conscript army is hot and complains constantly of the insects and the lack of entertainments. Anybody in need of a whorehouse would need to return to Felipe Carrillo Puerto, and the only occasional sight is of tourist yachts off the coast. Today Vigia Chico, chicle's own entrepôt, is not so much hated as it is neglected; it hardly appears on the map.

Chachoben—The Chicle Camp as Heritage Tourism

In some places the visibility of chewing gum's history is now much more in evidence. Finally, the prospect of making money from the vestiges of the chicle economy has persuaded investors to create a theme park, like those dedicated to tropical marine life (Xell-Ha, Xcaret, Tres Rios, and many more) that have grown along the coast. A theme park dedicated to chicle is being planned.

The state government of Quintana Roo has announced its intention to invest significant sums of money in a "chicle camp"—an imitation camp built along the lines of those described in Ramón Beteta's *Tierra del Chicle* (see chapter 4). The chosen location for the camp, Chachoben, is the site of a village that was a *real* camp, inland from the southern coast, near the main coast road. This road is currently being widened into a six-lane freeway, and it stretches all the way from Tulum south to Chetumal. Near the turnoff to Chachoben another surfaced road is being built that runs to the Caribbean, almost sixty miles away. This part of the coast is the last frontier of the Mexican Caribbean coast, relatively free of development.

The chicle camp is expected to receive thousands of visitors from the coast nearby. The resorts of Mahajual and Xkalak, formerly important for their copra plantations and almost destroyed by Hurricane Janet in 1955, are being developed for the new market in cruise ship tourism. At the moment, their clientele is almost exclusively made up of scuba divers and sport fishers. First, however, both places have to be put on the electric grid. The idea is that tourists from cruise ships, and others visiting the southern coast, should visit Chachoben to imbibe something of the past. Constructing a chicle camp for tourists seemed to be the answer to a deficit of things for tourists to do in the area.

JungleGum—A New Sustainable Product?

Since the Internet was established as a global medium of communication, there have been various attempts to market sustainable goods and services using the Web. One of these is the organization JungleGum (http://www.junglegum.com), based in Gainesville,

Florida. On its Web site JungleGum introduces the reader to the history of chicle, the jungles from which it is sourced, and the life and work of chicleros. It offers a variety of chicle-based gums, which can be bought from the Web and which are guaranteed as organic chicle resin. It notes that the chicle industry had all but disappeared by 1980, even though the retail business of $140 million (U.S.) in 1942 (before synthetics) with sales of more than 1.5 billion in 1986. This enormous growth is largely attributable to synthetic gums, and only a tiny proportion of the sales by 1980 were chicle.

The organic industry makes the point that, in the past, both the quality of chicle delivered to the buyer and the quantity available from the forest were primary concerns of the industry. One of the most awkward problems that large manufacturers like Wrigley's encountered during the height of the chicle boom was that the chicle delivered to the United States was frequently contaminated with latex from other species of trees (at least one of them was the toxic *Metopium brownei*). Some chicleros would even put stones in the center of the *marquetas* (blocks) of gum to increase their weight. These measures of interference created impurities and thus irregularities in processing.

Organic producers claim that impurities are no longer a problem for two reasons. First, if they occur they can easily be traced since the market is so much smaller than it was in the past, and producers can easily be identified. Second, among the few buyers of natural chicle, their price can only be maintained by giving attention to quality. To do otherwise would mean to risk losing their contracts with the manufacturers. As demand for chicle is relatively low at present, all chicle can currently be sourced from forests where the species are abundant and of high quality. If demand were to rise, of course, this

The Rio Hondo, the border between Mexico and Belize

guarantee of quality might be jeopardized, as contractors would push farther into forests where first-class chicle is less abundant. In addition, the increase in demand might stimulate the old problems of overtapping—either too frequently or from immature trees.

During the last decade (1990–2000) only about two thousand tons of chicle were harvested annually (compared with about ten thousand tons at the height of the boom). Most of the demand, moreover, has come from the Far East, especially Japan, where consumers were prepared to pay premium prices for a natural, organic product. In a depleted market, the Japanese and Korean exports held some promise for the future. Unfortunately, the downturn in the Japanese economy since the late 1990s has seriously undermined the demand for natural chicle, and most of the warehouses have retained large unsold stocks.

Since 2000 there has been a growth in interest in natural chewing gum, although it is still incipient rather than real. The enthusiasm for chicle, prompted by the Internet, stems from the fact that it might form part of more sustainable forest systems and could be marketed and branded as a sustainable product. It is not difficult to satisfy a new generation of chewing gum customers who desire organic products, and advertising and marketing have emphasized this. Nevertheless, to obtain the necessary certification as a sustainable and fair-trade product is much more difficult. First the market has to be researched and developed, and only then can producers expect the kind of job security that will revitalize their production. Chicle might follow chocolate and some timber products in finding a reliable market of consumers who are primarily interested in the conditions under which it is produced, as well as its taste and organic properties. If and when that happens this book will need to go into a revised edition.

ENDNOTES

Chapter 1

1. As Michel Foucault expressed it, the body can be seen as a "dense transfer point" for ideas about power and progress; the body condenses meanings, relations, and values. M. Foucault, *The History of Sexuality* (1978).
2. Unofficially, gum had gone into space even earlier. Astronauts Major James A. McDivett and Major Edward H. White II had smuggled chewing gum on board their space capsule before blasting off on the *Gemini IV* mission. It was reported that Ed White lost his toothbrush during a walk in space, and the gum helped keep their mouths fresh. Assurances were given that they had then swallowed the gum. The more serious point, perhaps, is that globalization has consumed places as well as products, just as the body itself consumes nature, what John Urry has called "corporeal travel." J. Urry, *The Tourist Gaze* (1999).
3. According to the *Diario de Yucatán* newspaper, quoting Merida's Registrar of Markets, there are 1,243 registered *vendedores ambulantes* in the city, more than half of whom work around the central market. This number is being augmented at the rate of about one hundred a week; most of the new traders are being relocated to other areas of the city. Officials admit that there is very little public support for the regulation of street sellers, since most people regard the *ambulantes* as making an honorable living. However, the report also suggested that the *ambulantes* themselves "believe they are the owners of the street, and for this reason occupy more space than is officially permitted, preferring to pay fines than be moved elsewhere." *Diario de Yucatán*, Merida, August 5, 2001. Interestingly, there are also a few street traders who sell natural chicle in

Merida, and there is a limited but increasing demand for the original product of the region.

Chapter 2

1. Chicozapote (*Manilkara zapota*) is a native tree of Mexico and Central America. The fruit is also known as *sapodilla;* the fleshy pulp was prized by the native Mayan population of the region and was used to make sapodilla custard. Chicle gum is derived from the resin of the tree, by cutting zigzags in the bark and tapping the tree, rather like conventional rubber. However, although the latex is a polyterpene, it does not vulcanize into durable rubber. (In 1839 Charles Goodyear accidentally spilled a mixture of rubber latex and sulfur on a hot stove and discovered that when it cooled the rubber lost its stickiness and retained its elasticity.)

2. The history of patent medicines illustrates the American conviction that you need to take the product to the market. By the late nineteenth century a number of factors combined to accelerate the mobility and visibility of the vendor, including the new transcontinental railroad, lower postal rates, an expanded popular daily press, and better advertising copy. "Patent-medicine makers were able to reach a market that spilled across a continent." David Armstrong and Elizabeth Metzger Armstrong, *The Great American Medicine Show* (New York: Prentice Hall, 1991), 163.

3. "As sugar became more known, more 'homey,' it was endowed with ritual meanings by those who consumed it, meanings specific to the social and cultural position of the users." Sidney Mintz, *Sweetness and Power: The Place of Sugar in Modern History* (New York: Penguin, 1986), 122.

4. The full quotation reads as follows:
   "No, I don't care for rats much, anyway. What I like is chewing gum," [said Tom Sawyer to Becky Thatcher].
   "Oh, I should say so. I wish I had some now."
   "Do you? I've got some. I'll let you chew it a while, but you must give it back to me."
   That was agreeable, so they chewed it turn about, and dangled their legs against a bench in excess of contentment. Mark Twain, *The Adventures of Tom Sawyer,* (1876).

5. Everyday items of consumption have not always been available, and their use was often much less than habitual. The banana is a case in point. Until the mid-nineteenth century, fresh fruit and vegetables were always eaten during the harvest season. However, in the 1890s, steamship and railroad networks expanded and brought tropical products to the American table, providing much needed vitamins and enriching the diet. As Virginia Scott Jenkins put it, "The idea of pricing bananas low enough so that everyone

could buy them and still make a profit for the producing company preceded Henry Ford's Model T." V. S. Jenkins, *Bananas: The American History* (Washington: Smithsonian Institution Press, 2000), 56. Several of the factors that came into play in widening the market for bananas closely paralleled those of chewing gum: low cost, around-the-year availability, ease of consumption, and distinctive taste. Like chewing gum, the introduction of bananas to the mass diet of the United States (and later Europe) was also a huge success for advertising. "Banana-eating was not a habit acquired from the people of Central America or Africa. Banana consumption in the United States was a marketing success largely attributable to the United Fruit Company. . . . [A]s bananas were assimilated into the diet in the United States, they were also being appropriated as American" (pp. 170–71).

6. Alexis de Tocqueville, *Democracy in America* (New York: Mentor, 1956), 210. Tocqueville's thesis was that Americans believed that emulation was possible, that nothing was forbidden them, in principle. Seventy years later Thorstein Veblen viewed these "democratic impulses" rather differently and argued that they were no barrier to the accumulation of private wealth nor, more particularly, to the pleasure that individuals gained from material inequality. Veblen saw that the majority could not consume "conspicuously," but those who could did. Successful entrepreneurs included the early chewing gum "barons," of course. T. Veblen, *The Theory of the Leisure Class* (New York: Mentor, 1953).

7. J. K. Galbraith, *Affluent Society* (1958), 194.

8. S. Lebergott, *Pursuing Happiness: American Consumers in the Twentieth Century* (Princeton, NJ: Princeton University Press, 1993). Lebergott made the point that most of things that constitute necessities bring us little pleasure as such. Food, clothes, and housing are covered in expectations that we imbibe socially and through vehicles like advertising. Consumption is driven by expectations, "which typically provide consumers with a mere ticket of admission to future experience" (p. 8).

9. The distinguished economist Nicholas Kaldor wrote in *Equilibrium Theory and Growth Theory* (1979) that equilibrium theory "takes the thoroughly misleading [view] that men have wants or needs" given by their nature "independently of the social environment and of the social institutions created for satisfying them" (pp. 273–74). Other perspectives are those of Johan Galtung, who sees the satisfaction of needs as both dependent on social structure and individual attainment (Galtung 1990). Doyal and Gough breathed life into social needs theory by linking the satisfaction of basic needs with empirical work on social indicators (Doyal and Gough 1991). All these approaches, unlike that of neoclassical economics, "fit the consumer whom [we] know personally much better than . . . the model of the solipsist sovereign rational consumer of economic theory, whose own shopping is for

his or her own consumption [alone]." Douglas et al. in Rayner and Malone, *Human Choice and Climate Change* (Columbus: Battelle Press, 2002), 252.

10. Christiane Harzig, "There Is No 'Kaiser' Here: The United States as a Country of Immigration," in *Fame, Fortune and Sweet Liberty: The Great European Emigration,* ed. D. Hoerder and D. Knauf (1992).
11. Ibid., 139.
12. Armstrong and Armstrong, *The Great American Medicine Show.*
13. "Horace Fletcher: The Great Masticator," in Armstrong and Armstrong, *The Great American Medicine Show.*
14. Armstrong and Armstrong, *The Great American Medicine Show,* 127.
15. Late-nineteenth-century American entrepreneurs often combined enormous tenacity with a touching lack of self-consciousness. Self-made millionaires found that once they had succeeded in their personal ambitions, their restless energy did not enable them to fit comfortably into the existing social structure. This was true not only of Hershey, who invented the chocolate bar, but also of Isaac Singer, who invented the sewing machine—one of the world's great popular inventions of the time. As Ruth Brandon wrote, "Time [after 1863] was just what he did have. . . . [H]e had occupied himself during the years between 1864 and 1875 with trying to identify a niche in society where this might most suitably be spent. He never completed his quest. He had identified various areas where he and his family were *not* acceptable: notably, respectable society in America and high society in England. Twenty years earlier such rebuffs would have been supremely unimportant to him." R. Brandon, *Singer and the Sewing Machine: A Capitalist Romance* (New York: Kodansha, 1977).
16. Betty Burford, *Chocolate by Hershey* (Minneapolis, Minn.: Lerner Publishing, 1994). See also the classic biographies by Catherine Shippen and Paul Wallace, *Milton S. Hershey* (New York: Random House, 1959), and Mary Malone, *Milton Hershey: Chocolate King* (Champaign, Ill.: Garrard Publishing, 1971).
17. Wrigley's life and work is well represented on the World Wide Web. The other leading references include Jospeh Gustaitis, "The Sticky History of Chewing Gum," *American History* (October 1998); Robert Young, *The Chewing Gum Book* (Minneapolis, Minn.: Dillon Press, 1989); and Lee Wardlaw, *Bubblemania: The Chewy History of Bubble Gum* (New York: Simon & Schuster, 1997). Wardlaw's book is particularly insightful and is aimed at children.

Chapter 3

1. The term *cacique* describes a local political boss or leader, usually in a rural area of Mexico, and vested with considerable, and usually unquestioned, personal authority.

2. Nelson Reed 2001.
3. Reed quotes the anthropologist Kroeber: "At this moment a prophet is likely to arise and picture a wish fulfillment; a release from the human impasse by supernatural mechanism" (Reed 2001, 147; Kroeber 1948).
4. The cenote is a sinkhole or well, which forms in the limestone of the region and, in the absence of rivers, is filled by underground streams. The cenote has enormous ceremonial and religious significance for the Maya.
5. Nelson Reed, 151.
6. Ibid., 186–87.
7. Nelson Reed, *The Caste War of Yucatán* (Stanford, Calif.: Stanford University Press, 1964). Reed's book is one of the most engaging, skillfully crafted, and insightful pieces of historical scholarship ever written. It is also extremely readable, indeed impossible to put down, and without it the current author would, like most people, have remained lost in the convolutions of historical events.
8. Nelson Reed 2001.
9. Ibid., Reed 2001.
10. Martin Ramos Diaz, "La bonanza del chicle en la frontera caribe de Mexico," *Revista Mexicana del Caribe* IV, no. 7 (1999): 172–93.
11. Ibid.
12. Herman Konrad, "Capitalism on the Tropical-Forest Frontier: Quintana Roo, 1880s to 1930s," in *Land, Labor and Capital in Modern Yucatán*, eds. Jeffery Brannon and Gilbert Joseph (Tuscaloosa: University of Alabama Press, 1991).
13. Porfirio Diaz was president of Mexico. His long period of office, which culminated in the Mexican Revolution, was one in which foreign capital was attracted into Mexico in an attempt to modernize the economy and society.
14. As ever, Nelson Reed's (2001) description of the conquest of Chan Santa Cruz is unparalleled: It was expected that General Bravo would take the enemy "capital" the first of April, but he seemed in no hurry, concentrating instead on the road and on bringing the telegraph line forward, day after day, week after week. And then the rains started. A traveling peddler from Valladolid, Alonso Villanueva, made his way to the final camp at Chan Kiwk carrying sugar, chocolate and candles for the fiesta of the Day of the Cross. His horse got loose during the night, and in the morning he followed its tracks through the woods to where it was grazing peacefully in an opening in the forest. While picking mangoes there he realized that the opening was in fact a street with half-hidden houses that led to a plaza and a large stone church, and that the church was the sanctuary of the Cruzob. He hurried back to the military camp and reported what he had seen. Two days later, early in the morning of May 4, Bravo led his men into Noh Cah Balam Na Santa Cruz. (pp. 299–300)
Subsequently the first ever photographs were taken of the rebel capital.
15. Konrad, 1991.

16. Ibid., 154.
17. The sanctity and respect paid to the Talking Cross has not diminished among believers even to this day. A recent letter published in the magazine *Nicte T'an*, an organ of Mayan cultural revival, criticized some of the local election candidates in Felipe Carrillo Puerto for using a (Christian) cross in their promotional literature. The writer argued that, among the devout Maya, it was sacrilegious to use this symbol for political purposes.
18. Reed 2001, 302. As many Mexican soldiers as Maya may have died in the pathetic attempts to round up the remaining rebels that followed, partly because of the appalling disease and sanitary conditions that prevailed in the forest.
19. Ibid., 304. Vigia Chico today consists of nothing but an isolated military post of the Mexican army.
20. Ibid., 304–305.
21. C. Anda Gutierrez, *Quintana Roo: Tres casos* (Mexico DF: Union Grafica, 1986). Another useful source on this period is L. Careaga Viliesid, *Quintana Roo: Entre la selva y el mar* (Mexico DF: Secretaria de Educacion Publica, 1982).
22. Reed (2001) noted that while he was in the capital, May made use of other facilities. "The General found himself a lady who exceeded all his backwoods dreams (in a house where there were other equally friendly ladies), and not content with a brief affair he decided to take her home. She got as far as Vigia Chico, where an unfriendly reception by the Maya convinced her that this trip was not a good idea. Back home, Pancho May unbuckled his ceremonial sword, took off his general's uniform, and set to work weeding his milpas with a machete" (pp. 309–10).
23. According to May's personal secretary, Felipe Neri Avila Zapata, May's authority was entirely consistent with that of the Mayan military general and ceremonial head, *el patron del santuario*. May did not die until 1969, and this account, in the magazine *Nicte T'an* (April 2001) relies, incredibly, on an interview with Neri himself.
24. Deprived of his control over the forests, taxation, and local justice, May expressed the wish to retire from public office, which he did in 1929. Lino Balam assumed leadership of the tribes. Some of the Mayan forces, under Evarista Sulub and Concepcion Cituk, entered the church in Chan Santa Cruz and took the cross and other reliquaries to the village of Xcacal Guardia, where they remain to this day. When General May died, on March 31, 1969, he was living in a modest house in Felipe Carrillo Puerto. However, he was buried in a luxurious coffin, which puzzled commentators at the time. After his death, a statue to him was erected, which depicts him looking westward, toward the sunset. Mario Chan Colli, "XXXII Aniversario luctuoso del General Francisco May," *Nicte T'an* (April 2001).
25. There is some evidence from recent fieldwork that the income from chicle increased inequality among the Maya of Quintana Roo. "The unequal

distribution of the profits from collecting chicle had been a reason for internal conflicts and the separation of the Txcacal group in 1929." Ramon Arzapalo Marin and Ruth Gubler, *Persistencia Cultural Entre Los Mayas Frente Al cambio y la Modernidad* (Ediciones Universidad de Yucatán, 1997), 19.

26. Konrad 1991, 162–63.

27. Reed (2001) noted that, after 1929, May received a pension, but this did not protect him from bankruptcy. The local custom was to bury gold and silver coins in the ground. Unfortunately when the land was cleared for a *milpa*, the stick showing where the coins were buried could not be located. More money had been left with his wife, who had died while he was in British Honduras. He assumed that she also had buried it, but there was no way of knowing where exactly. May's fortunes declined and eventually he was exiled from Noh Cah Balam Na Santa Cruz. As Reed wrote, "In fourteen years he had gone through several transformations: from militant independent leader, to the wealthy director of his tribe's prosperity in the chicle boom, to desperate negotiator with Mexico's civil and military government, to penniless exile" (p. 321).

28. Ramos Diaz (1999) made the point that the lucrative trade prolonged divisions between the various Mayan leaders, who each made contracts with different white or *mestizo* intermediaries, and fought when they thought their sovereignty over sections of the forest was being violated.

29. Quoted by Ramos Diaz (1999). Konrad (1991) made the point that the Cruzoob had not fully understood the implications of becoming so dependent on chicle. Their main livelihood activities, the *milpa*, supplemented by hunting and gathering, were adversely affected by the chicle boom. "Gathering chicle and guerrilla fighting were almost mutually exclusive activities" (p. 165) as the Maya found themselves with hoards of gold coins but fewer people willing to fight. As the fighting diminished, the need to purchase more weapons diminished also. The commerce, whose initial attraction to the Maya had been that of financing armaments, ended by making armaments less necessary, or attractive, to the Maya.

30. "By 1937 chicle production in Quintana Roo was practically socialized in its totality." *Encyclopedia of Quintana Roo*, vol. III (1998), 98.

31. Anda Gutierrez 1982, 116.

32. Most of this was exported to just three American companies: Beech Nut of New Jersey (30 percent), Wrigley's of Chicago (28 percent), and the American Chicle Company of Long Island, New York (23 percent).

33. *Encyclopedia of Quintana Roo*, 102.

34. The literature on the Caste War is now very extensive, especially following the pioneering work of Nelson Reed, *The Caste War of Yucatán*. In 2001 a revised edition of Reed's classic appeared. See also Victoria Bricker, *The Indian Christ, the Indian King* (Austin: University of Texas Press, 1981); Terry Rugeley, *Yucatán's Peasantry and the Origins of the Caste War* (Austin:

University of Texas Press, 1996); Jeffery Brannon and Gilbert Joseph, eds., *Land, Labor, and Capital in Modern Yucatán: Essays in Regional History and Political Economy* (Tuscaloosa: University of Alabama Press, 1991); Alfonso Villa Rojas, *The Maya of East Central Quintana Roo* (Washington, DC: Carnegie Institution of Washington, 1945); Don Dumond, *The Machete and the Cross* (Lincoln: University of Nebraska Press, 1997); P. Sullivan, *Unfinished Conversations: Mayas and Foreigners between Two Wars* (New York: Knopf, 1989).

35. In the new edition of his 2001 work Reed detailed various meetings he had with Cruzoob in the villages that still remain faithful to the cross. During 2001 and 2002 I visited several of these, including Txcacal Guardia and Xocen, and found that while people were willing to talk about the ways in which the cross was celebrated, they were highly suspicious of outsiders' interest in their movement.

Chapter 4

1. The process described is the one followed during the period of chicle boom in the 1920s and 1930s. Various changes have taken place since, in both the harvesting and production of raw chicle, but the details are accurate for the period under discussion.

2. The closest group to that of the chicleros is probably that of the rubber tappers in the Brazilian Amazon, the *seringueiros*, whose struggle for freedom under Chico Mendes is well documented. See *Fight for the Forest: Chico Mendes in His Own Words* (London: Latin American Bureau, 1989); Stephen Schwartzman, "Extractive Reserves: The Rubber Tappers; Strategy for Uustainable Use of the Amazon Rainforest," in *Fragile Lands of Latin America*, ed. John O. Browder (Boulder, CO: Westview Press, 1989); A. Hall, "Did Chico Mendes Die in Vain: Brazilian Rubber Tappers in the 1990s," in *Green Guerrillas: Environmental Conflicts and Initiatives in Latin America and the Caribbean*, ed. Helen Collinson (London: Latin American Bureau, 1996).

3. *The Clarion*, November 16, 1905, quoted in *Encyclopedia of Quintana Roo* (p. 216).

4. Beteta died in October 1965, several years before the territory of Quintana Roo became a Mexican state.

5. Moises Saenz, in the introduction to the 1951 edition (*Tierra del Chicle,* 21).

6. Ibid., 31.

7. Ibid., 34. The inhospitality of the forest is in contrast to accounts of settlers in more benign forest environments, such as Upper Canada in the 1840s. See M. R. Redclift, *The Frontier Environment and Social Order: The Letters of Francis Codd from Upper Canada* (Chichester, UK: Edward Elgar, 2000).

8. Beteta, 37.
9. Ibid., 42–43.
10. Ibid., 65.
11. The situation in Calakmul is described in Nora Haenn, "Nature Regimes in Southern Mexico: A History of Power and Environment," *Ethnology* 41, no. 1 (2002), who in turn draws on M. Ponce Jimenez, *Montana chiclera Campeche: Vida cotidiana y trabajo (1900–1950)* (Mexico DF) for her description of the first half of the twentieth century. Ponce Jimenez's study is one of the few to rest squarely on the oral accounts of chicleros and their families.
12. Haenn, 10.
13. Jorge Gonzalez Duran, *La Rebelion de los mayas y el Quintana Roo chiclero* (Merida: Editorial Dosis, 1974).
14. See Peter Klepeis, who called the first model the Diaz model, after President Diaz (the prerevolutionary Mexican president), and the second model the Cardenas model, using these terms throughout the postrevolutionary period. In practice, successive Mexican governments used combinations of these approaches, partly depending on available funds, partly their dependence on peasant clientalism, and partly on Mexico's external economic position (Klepeis et al. 2001).
15. Ibid., p. 15.
16. This point is well illustrated by Klepeis in his work.
17. Bridge wrote that social and geographical spaces like those of Quintana Roo are "simultaneously emptied and filled . . . tropes of blankness and emptiness [that] are used to denote social emptiness and a location outside history" (Bridge 2001).

Chapter 5

1. *Dentyne* was a hybrid of *dental* and *hygiene*, and the term was coined to emphasize the benefits of chewing gum for the teeth and oral hygiene.
2. Lee Wardlaw, *Bubblemania: The Chewy History of Bubble Gum* (New York: Simon & Schuster, 1997).
3. Indeed, in 1937 the Japanese government complained to the United States when the Bowman company featured a card that depicted the atrocities committed by their troops in China. The Japanese had recently sunk a U.S. gunboat on the Yangtze River, and the State Department was in no mood to concur with Japanese demands. By 1935 more than $1 million's worth of chewing gum was being sold to China annually (Wardlaw 1997).
4. Wardlaw (1997, 52) quoted this anecdote in her excellent book for kids.
5. Franz A. Koehler, "Army Operational Rations from the Revolutionary War to the End of World War II," in *Historical Studies,* series II, no. 6, *Historical Branch* (Washington, DC: Office of the Quartermaster General, 1958).

6. Herbert R. Rifkind, *Fresh Foods for the Armed Forces,* no. 20, *QMC Historical Studies* (Washington, DC: 1951); Elliott Cassidy, *The Development of Meat, Dairy, Poultry and Fish Products for the Army,* no. 7, *QMC Historical Studies* (Washington, DC: 1944); Harold W. Thatcher, *The Development of Special Rations for the Army,* no. 6, *QMC Historical Studies* (Washington, DC: 1944).

7. See D. E. Goodman and M. R. Redclift, *Refashioning Nature: Food Ecology and Culture* (London: Routledge, 1991).

8. Rifkind.

9. Ibid., 17.

10. David Reynolds, *Rich Relations: The American Occupation of Britain* (London: HarperCollins, 1996).

11. Ibid., 434.

12. According to British Mass Observation, this view of the Americans was mixed: Older people were much less pro-American. One middle-aged woman from a rural part of the country commented, "Every time I see an American soldier slouching along, hands in his pockets, shoulders hunched, chewing gum, I'm glad I'm not an American" (Reynolds 1996, 435).

13. David Cannadine, *G. M. Trevelyan: A Life in History* (London: 1992), 175.

14. Reynolds 1996, 438.

15. Reynolds (1996) reminded us that many of the American G.I.s were very young, barely out of their teens themselves, far from home and acutely home-sick. The romance attached to their appearance in an old country was partly of their own making, but also a very bored population of young women expected to spend their time working and obeying their elders attached a label to them. As Reynolds put it, "There were more young men walking the towns—more evident because they wore strange uniforms, spoke with different accents, and had money to throw about. The disruption of family life, especially for females, meant that there were more unaccompanied women on the streets and in the pubs, all through the week, while sexual encounters could be more public because of the privacy of the blackout" (p. 276).

16. Ibid., 266.

17. *Encyclopedia* 101.

18. C. Anda Gutierrez, *Quintana Roo: Tres casos* (Mexico City: Union Grafica, 1986), and L. Careaga Viliesid, *Quintana Roo: Entre selva y el mar* (Mexico City: SEP, 1982).

Chapter 6

1. F. Scott Fitzgerald, *Tender Is the Night* (New York: Scribner, 1962), 54–55.

2. David Nye has explored this area with great originality in his work. He wrote,

Early in the nineteenth century, theater, symphonic music, and opera were democratically shared in the popular culture. In the second half of the century, however, each was gradually "elevated" to an art form. Attending performances became costly, texts were rigorously edited to eliminate many popular features, and these art forms were endowed with high moral seriousness. Earlier concerts and plays had presented an "eclectic feast" of genres, but by 1900 a severe classicism reigned. Shakespeare had been converted from a popular playwright whose dramas were the property of those who flocked to see them, into a scared author who had to be protected from ignorant audiences and overbearing actors threatening the integrity of his creations. D. Nye, *Consuming Power: A Social History of American Energies* (Cambridge, Mass.: MIT Press, 1999.)

Nye went on to compare this process with the way in which popular audiences transferred their preferences to new cultural products, such as fireworks, baseball, carnivals, electric fountains, and amusement arcades.

3. "It may well be that one opera house in a middle-sized American town in the 1880s offered more of the classic tradition of music and drama in one year than the combined television networks of the United States does in the same period of time in our own age." H. Wayne Morgan, ed., *The Gilded Age: A Reappraisal* (New York: Syracuse University Press, 1963), 173.

4. One of the most important aspects of mass consumption and twentieth-century popular culture was the increasing visibility of the product and the increasing invisibility of the labor from which the product was drawn. An example of this process—and one that soon assumed enormous importance in popular culture—was the role of photography in the new society. The new visual imagery created by photography was put to work in the first mass society of the twentieth century. This took the form of a democratization of the camera image. The link between industrial labor and the new popularity of photography is explored by Naomi and Walter Rosenblum: The conflict in Europe in 1914 signaled the end of the great labor migrations to the United States. Though industrial capacity continued to expand to meet both [World War I] demands and the growing interest in automobile transportation . . . standardization, along with newly rationalized methods of industrial production . . . created systems that turned individual workers into cogs, while promising investors more profitable returns. Advertising, an emerging field at the time, also abetted the concentration on product and process rather than on labor. This enterprise, which turned to photographic images of mass-produced commodities as more convincing than graphic depiction, was eager to set forth the material aspects of American capitalist technology rather than to suggest that these products were the result of human effort. N. Rosenblum and W. Rosenblum, "Camera Images of Labor—Past and Present," in *The Other America,* eds. Philip S. Foner and Reinhardt Schultz (London: Journeyman Press, 1985), 110.

5. Mintz (1986) referred to this process as a recasting of meanings, as items of consumption become a part of everyday consumer practice. He drew a contrast between continuity in the ritual meanings of things, which he called *intensification*, and the more frequent and greater consumption of new additions to everyday life, which he termed *extensification*. It is interesting to reflect on the parallels with sugar itself an important component of chewing gum, which Mintz discusses. Sugar moved down the social hierarchy, but chicle had always been a popular product, even before the commercial production of chewing gum. In the case of gum, meanings were recast at the point it acquired exchange value, rather than through the evolution of different markets for the product.

6. S. A. Marston, "The Social Construction of Scale," *Progress in Human Geography* 24 (2000): 219–41.

7. J. Agnew, "Mapping Political Power beyond State Boundaries: Territory, Identity and the Movement in World Politics," *Millennium* 28 (1999): 499–521.

8. Wittgenstein, quoted in Nigel Thrift, "Afterwords," *Environment and Planning D* 18 (2000): 213–23.

9. Bridge 2001, 2155.

10. Perhaps "we need to consider the discursive marginality of these spaces. Not as the result of a collective act of forgetting, but as a specific encoding and performance of the social power to organize space" (Bridge 2001, 2155).

11. D. Held, *Democracy and the Global Order* (Cambridge: Polity Press, 1995). Globalization "is a process which embodies a transformation in the spatial organization of social relations and transactions—assessed in terms of their extensity, intensity, velocity, and impact—generating transcontinental or interregional flows and networks of activity, interaction, and the exercise of power." D. Held, A. McGrew, D. Goldblatt, and J. Perraton, *Global Transformations* (Cambridge: Polity Press, 1999), 16.

12. Ash Amin, "Spatialities of Globalization," *Environment and Planning A* 34 (2002): 385–99.

13. A. Herod and M. W. Wright, "Theorizing Space and Time," *Environment and Planning A* 33 (2001): 2089.

14. Deleuze, see Thrift, "Afterwords".

15. In the case of tobacco, these new markets opened up among young women in the past two or three decades, in the developed world, as the incidence of smoking among men declined markedly. Internationally major expansion has occurred in the new markets of Asia. Mathew Hilton, *Smoking in British Popular Culture 1800–2000* (Manchester: Manchester University Press, 2000).

16. William Gervase Clarence-Smith, *Cocoa and Chocolate 1765–1914* (London and New York: Routledge, 2000). See also Betty Burford, *Chocolate by Hershey* (Minneapolis, Minn.: Lerner Publishing, 1994).

17. It has proved difficult for chewing gum manufacturers to penetrate local and national markets where chewing was a well-established indigenous tradition, notably India and the Horn of Africa.

18. Gavin Bridge, "Resource Triumphalism: Post-Industrial Narratives of Primary Commodity Production," *Environment and Planning A* 33 (2002): 759–66.

19. An interesting contrast is that with travel. John Urry, "Mobility and Proximity," *Sociology* 36 (May 2002): 2.

Chapter 7

1. Alfredo Cesar Dachary and Stella Maris Arnaiz Burne, *El Caribe Mexicano: Una frontera olvidada* (Mexico: University of Quintana Roo, 1998). Maurie Cohen and Joseph Murphy, eds., "Changing Nature: The Consumption of Space and the Construction of Nature on the 'Mayan Riviera'" in *Sustainable Consumption* (Elsevier, 2001).

2. Michael Redclift, "Changing Nature: the Consumption of Space and the Construction of Nature on the 'Mayan Riviera'" in Maurie Cohen and Joseph Murphy (eds.), *Sustainable Consumption* (Elsevier, 2001).

3. These reserves are Sian Khan, on the southern coast, north of Belize, and Calakmul; the vast are of tropical forest inland that extends into Guatemala in the Grand Peten. The history of conservation in Mexico is outlined in L. Simonian, *Defending the Land of the Jaguar: A History of Conservation in Mexico* (Austin: University of Texas Press, 1995).

4. C. Kallen, "Eco-Tourism: The Light at the End of the Tunnel," *E-Magazine* (July/August 1990). Also compare the views of J. Croall, *Preserve or Destroy: Tourism and the Environment* (London: Gulbenkian Foundation, 1995); S. Wahab and J. J. Pigram, *Tourism, Development and Growth: The Challenge of Sustainability* (New York: Routledge, 1997); Arturo Carballo Sandoval, "Community Involvement in Sustainable Ecotourism: The Case of the Mexican Caribbean Area" (geographical paper, no. 140, University of Reading, 1999).

5. John L. Stephens, *Incidents of Travel in Yucatán,* vols. I and II, 1st condensed ed. (panorama editorial, Mexico City, 1988).

6. Martin Ramos Diaz, "La bonanza del chicle en la frontera caribe de Mexico: Indigenas ye empresarios, 1918–1930," *Revista Mexican del Caribe* IV, no. 7 (1999): 172–93.

7. Reed 2001, p. 301.

8. Ibid., p. 304.

INDEX